THE BEST

LESSONS TO TRANSFORM YOUR LIFE

THE BEST U

LESSONS TO TRANSFORM YOUR LIFE

SHERYL CORRIVEAU

The Best U
Lessons to Transform Your Life

Cover designer: Sherwin Soy
Interior designer: Pamela Morrell

Title ID: 9154398

ISBN-13: 978-1727502916

Createspace Publishing

Sheryl Corriveau
774-254-1146
www.sherylcorriveau.com

To my daughter Mia

Ask and it will be given to you; seek and you will find; knock and the door will be opened to you. For everyone who asks receives; he who seeks finds and to him who knocks, the door will be opened.

—Matthew 7:7-8

ACKNOWLEDGEMENTS

I'd like to express my love and gratitude to the following people:

My daughter Mia, for being by far one of my greatest teachers of all… love you more than words can say.

Paula Sullivan, for lovingly being my north star, friend, and amazing mentor on this writing journey!!

Nancy Anger, for teaching me how to live by my "full body yes"!

To my mom and dad, for everything.

Karen Moriarty, for making me look so good!

Jon VanZile, for your honesty, insight, and patience as my editor!

For the people in my life who have shaped my mind, soul, and spirit that I haven't mentioned, thank you all.

INTRODUCTION

This book has been inside waiting to be born for quite some time. You've probably heard it before: "one day" or "day one"...so here's day one. Most of my life I lived with an uncomfortable feeling that there was more to life than I understood. I craved the truth beneath the surface. It's always fascinated me to understand how life works. When I was younger, I inwardly questioned much of the reality behind many things I was told. Being raised a Catholic, it was a given to not question, do what you're told (which is always the "right thing"), and be good—or you're basically going to hell. Guess I was on my way there because, feeling confused and unguided, I certainly had some rebellious and wild teenage years in a way that I can't help but shake my head at today.

Wanting to live my truth has been a thread to a greater or lesser degree throughout the years. The flip side of this was that, for a long time, I never felt quite as peaceful as I desired, and I had many turbulent relationships—including the one with myself. Again, I questioned why this was so. Why did some people lead happy lives while others did not? Why were some people successful while others were not? Why were some people peaceful inside and others were not? Eventually this began the journey to finding answers by reading, studying, and researching what made the difference in how our lives turn out. A pattern became clear: our minds hold the power that influences the quality of our lives. Being unable to resist my own curiosity and passion for the truth, I finally surrendered to the realization that if I was to change my life, I needed to take 100 percent responsibility. Understanding that my mind held the key, I began working on myself like a full-time job. After giving myself permission to unapologetically live my own truth, many aspects of my life improved as my awareness of what life was all about began to change.

In April 2004, I had my daughter. This gift I've been fortunate enough to experience touched me deeply. To this day, my daughter has given me tons of perspective on the meaning of life itself, which I believe is love. Loving others is one of life's greatest gifts. Loving yourself is a way of expressing reverence for this amazing life. The art of taking care of the most priceless gift we've been given—our life—is what this book is about.

In 2005, I started a small Pilates business, and in 2010 I graduated from the Institute for Integrative Nutrition (IIN), as a health coach. These two modalities helped me to heal by helping others heal and improve their lives. So much of my path was showing me that we all deal with human emotions, feelings, strengths, and weaknesses, and it's how we learn how to handle them that makes all the difference. I realized the most important relationship I had to understand and improve was the one with myself. This self-seeking led to many teachers who had similar paths with their own struggles. Louise Hay, Marianne Williamson, Jim Rohn, Wayne Dyer, Tony Robbins, Gabrielle Bernstein, Les Brown and John Kehoe are only a few...but honestly, there are so many others who I am forever grateful to for being transparent and sharing their own story. Collectively, they inspired me to know that it was possible to change my own life too.

It takes continued effort and daily choices to live with intention and love. Now I can say that I'm truly grateful for all of the valleys I've experienced. If not for them, I would've never been so driven to learn or honestly willing to change myself.

For those ready and needing to hear it, this book will feel like a freedom pass to honor your power and create your life the way you choose. It comes down to knowing our gifts, learning how to create more value, setting clear intentions, living from the end of our ideal outcomes, deciding YES for persistence and NO to negative energy thoughts and time wasters, learning to constantly test and change (which is what all life is), and giving yourself the permission to soar and be the 100 percent authentic best version of yourself you can be. It's about taking control of YOU and letting go of what you can't.

These have been my life's lessons. They have taken many years to learn and continue to shape my perspective on how to navigate three elements: my mind, my energy, and my time. How I manage these elements makes all the difference in the experiences that show up. I chose to take back my power a long time ago because I didn't care for how I had managed my life and the experiences I had as a result. We've all experienced pain, and that's part of being human, but I strongly believe we can minimize much of it by accepting that we have a creative force inside of us that can be awakened and used to create immense change and great fulfillment if we dare. My wish for you is to live your life to the fullest and regret nothing.

In this book, I'll share the wisdom that has totally reshaped my life. Since all of life is a school, if you apply these lessons, it is my promise that they can change yours too!

—**Sheryl**

CONTENTS

THE LESSON OF CREATING

"You are one thing only. You are a Divine Being. An all-powerful Creator. You are a Deity in jeans and a T-shirt, and within you dwells the infinite wisdom of the ages and the sacred creative force of All that is, will be and ever was."

—Anthon St. Maarten

To create is to bring something into existence. Throughout this book, I will show how to understand and embrace the fact that this is who you are: a creator of your life. Learning how to fully own this amazing power is where we start.

Merriam-Webster's dictionary defines creating as "to bring into existence."

There was a time when my life was a real mess. I was twenty-eight and pregnant, and the impregnator had left me. I was freaked out and had no idea how I was going to do this on my own.

Seeking guidance, I found myself driving to a place called La Salette Shrine. I think a part of me wanted to go somewhere where I wouldn't know anyone. When I got there, I spoke to a priest who gave me contact information for a counselor who offered advice for pregnant women.

A couple days later, I drove out to meet her. After explaining my predicament, she recommended I visit a place she knew that might be an option in my situation. It was a Christian shelter for pregnant women. *Big inhale.*

After visiting the shelter, there was a lot of processing going on in my head. The thought of a *shelter* brought sad images. I'd always assumed they were for skid row, down-and-out people, or folks who were using the system. The truth is, I didn't really know anyone who'd ever been in a shelter. I had some prejudices. I knew I wasn't looking to do anything against my conscience. I also knew I needed help. Fortunately, this place didn't match the images in my mind. It wasn't like that. For whatever reason, I felt a peace inside.

Finally, I made a decision. I gave up my apartment, car, and both of my jobs. I moved into Friends of the Unborn in Quincy. This is where I spent most of my pregnancy. Never in my wildest dreams did I think that living in a shelter would be part of my story.

Then I got the news. At five months pregnant, a test showed my baby had gastroschisis. This is a birth defect of the abdominal (belly) wall. The baby's intestines are outside of the baby's body, exiting through a hole beside the belly button. The hole can be small or large. Sometimes other organs, like the stomach and liver, can also be found outside of the baby's body.

There is no telling the severity until the baby is born. The best case is surgery after birth and the baby heals and goes on to live a healthy life. The worst case is death. The doctor, knowing my situation, recommended an abortion. At five months.

Was this really even happening? Bigger inhale.

This was by far one of the most challenging times in my life. Looking back, I can see that living in that shelter during this time was really a shelter for my spirit. I could have easily given into fear and the worst-case scenario. Except for the ladies. The ladies who ran the shelter were like angels. They talked and prayed with me. They had tons of faith. At the time, I was exactly where I needed to be.

I said no to the abortion and got a different doctor. Some people back home didn't agree with my decision. Everything felt like it was being ripped apart at the seams. Part of me was gone. It was such a surreal time.

Any form of safety seemed to have disappeared. My new constant companion was a deep unknowing. It was a time when the old me died. I wasn't even sure of who I was anymore.

Every morning at 5 a.m., I'd go upstairs to the chapel. I craved the quiet and solitude I found there. I'd do my mat Pilates routine and pray. For the first time in my life, there was no one's advice to take. No one could solve this one for me. There was no lightheartedness in my normally good-natured spirit. I didn't know what *normal* even was anymore.

I remember feeling like Lieutenant Dan in *Forrest Gump*, when he was at the top of the ship in that storm. He was yelling at God, just like me. My exact words were, "Either you're real, or I'm fucking crazy! I'm in one hell of a mess here, and I need a miracle! Show me what you got."

This was the moment that I learned what faith really was. It was the moment I stopped looking for outside opinions. I began a relationship with my Higher Power. It was within this relationship that I began to ask (finally) for wisdom and guidance. I went straight to the top of something bigger than me. There was no pride left in me at this point. I knew there was no way out except through. What I needed was a full-on miracle.

God became more real than anything I'd ever learned God was before this point. The Catholic God I grew up with was something outside of myself and judgmental. This *friend* was very different. It began as a cry of desperation, but it ended up becoming the greatest relationship in my life.

Sometimes I call God the Source, Universe, Inner Guide, or Higher Power. For me, it's all the same. Past all the illusions and fear, I found my strength. And I found myself.

When I look back to that time, it feels like a lifetime ago. I've grown and changed so much since then. I'm grateful and give thanks every day for the miracles I've witnessed along the way. What I know for sure is that during morning in the chapel of that shelter, a part of me came alive that had never breathed before. I needed to grow up. I needed to dig deeper into my spirit and learn how to go there, instead of seeking solace in people and things.

An inner strength was born. And so was my little girl. After my C-section, she had the surgery. We lived at Children's Hospital for just over a month, and then I brought her home. She did so well they actually used her as a case study.

My parents graciously offered for us to stay with them until I got on my feet. I used this time to earn three levels of Pilates certifications and become a personal trainer. My parents helped watch my daughter, enabling me to do these things. I'm forever grateful. My goal was that, within a year, I'd be back on my own with my daughter. I reached that goal…and many more since then.

Through this experience, I realized that what had gotten me to such a low place were the low standards I'd set for myself. I had low standards with men, my time and energy, and especially with my beliefs about how worthy and deserving I was. I had to pay a very high price to learn how to set higher standards. Life had gotten my full attention.

I craved learning. I was determined to understand how to rise up and live life smarter. I had a new respect for its inherent laws. From that time to this day, I haven't stopped working on myself.

Raising your standards is the key to living life as the best version of yourself. I believe it's about embracing the person you become along your journey. It's about always striving to improve your understanding of how to get just a little bit better every day.

Although this was my experience, I'm sure you have your own experience that's brought you in directions you never thought you'd go. These experiences show you where you'd like to improve. Through them, you're shown clearly what you want and what you don't. No matter how much you mess up, it doesn't mean you're a mess-up! We all make mistakes. Sometimes our mistakes also become our miracles.

Part of being human is that life is super messy. Don't beat yourself up any more than you already have! Just get up and *decide* to change for the better. Taking responsibility is the only way to improve your life. Learning how to manage being the amazing creator of life that you are meant to be takes acquiring certain skills. For many years, I didn't have these skills, and my life reflected it back to me. Thankfully, the school of hard knocks woke me up. Hopefully, sharing what I've learned the hard way will help you save time and energy, so that you can focus on being the best version of you.

Each and every day, there must be an intentional time set aside to nourish the aspects of yourself that show up as the best creator possible.

FIVE QUESTIONS TO IDENTIFY A LACK OF CREATING

1. Are you happy with your current life experience?
2. If you knew how, would you do better?
3. Do you often need other's approval before you move ahead with plans?
4. Do you have so many ideas of what you'd like to do that it's hard to pick one and get started?
5. Do you often dream of a better life, but it always feels out of reach?

These questions are meant to help you look at your life from different angles. When you become an active creator for your best self, you're ready to raise your standards. Creating is about growing into who you become on your journey. Growing happens on whatever level your currently on. Then it moves to another level…and another. You can create amazing things when you believe in yourself!

FIVE METHODS TO CREATE BETTER

1. Raise Your Energy Daily

Exercise daily to raise your energy to a higher level. Period. There are so many ways to move, but try to think of whatever exercise you choose as any other relationship. Creating a habit of exercise means you must match it to your current physical condition. Do what will challenge you, but also what's safe for your level of fitness. Secondly, you must commit. This means making it a daily appointment. And third, it must fit into your life as something you can do regularly. Take a look at your schedule, and make this appointment one that fits at a time you'll be able to regularly honor.

Mornings have always been the best time for me because it sets the tone for the rest of the day. I've always been into Pilates, but I also realized I needed some cardio to get my sweat on and my heart pumping. So I signed up for Beachbody on Demand because it worked for my busy lifestyle, and I could do it at home before the day got started. For the record, I'm not into Beachbody for the business, but I do recommend it as a way to add variety without taking the time to drive to a gym. There are a ton of YouTube videos for free. Of course, a gym may be perfect for you. Be open to whatever works best for your time and schedule. Like Nike says, *Just Do It!*

Exercise changes your state of mind, increases your metabolism, keeps you strong mentally and physically, and let's face it, who doesn't want to look good? When you're purposely setting out to create your life to support the best version of yourself, the body you live in can't be neglected. When your body's run down, tired, or sick, you're not going to feel like your best self. It requires investing in yourself from a high level of love and respect.

My friend in her forties had never run a day in her life. She started out with small, manageable runs. Over time, her mind adjusted to the fact that *she could run!* Before this, she had a mental obstacle that prevented her from even trying. She'd told herself, "I can't run like other people." It was so crazy that she believed this lie, but it was a story that had been running in her head for years. Now she loves that she got past that lie, and she's found a new relationship with running. The best part is that while she's raising her energy, she's also creating a new, empowering story about what she's capable of. Raising the standard about what you believe is possible for you, in any area of your life, affects every other area.

Exercise is an essential ingredient in raising your energy. Once your energy is raised, you are able to create from a much higher vibrational frequency! This is huge because while creating itself can make you feel great, it also requires a constant supply of energy. Energy is life. To raise your energy, embrace movement. Think of it as the wind that will fan your energy's fire.

2. Don't Wait for Things to Be Perfect

I wish I'd learned long ago that it's not a good idea to wait till things are perfect before beginning something. Fear can mask itself in many ways, and one of them is procrastinating because *everything's not perfect*. This held me back for so long…even with this book. I realized, however, that you have to get going before you can get good. Sure, sometimes things will come easily with hardly any effort, but I don't believe this will yield a satisfying and fulfilling life. There must be a willingness to do whatever you can, from exactly where you are, and with exactly what you have. Period.

If there's something inside of you that wants to be expressed, you need to do it! It can be a dream of changing careers, getting in the best shape of your life, writing a book, starting a new relationship, becoming a blogger, starting your own business, or traveling. It doesn't matter what it is, but if it's in you, there is a reason. Sometimes we just need to get something out of our system. You might find it's even better than you thought—or worse—or just have a chapter or two of it in your life before you move on. The point is, you are a creator. Even if you don't think you're creating, trust me that you are. By your thoughts, you're constantly forming experiences.

A few years ago, I was sitting at my kitchen table with my iPad. I was playing with the idea of what it would be like get my real estate license. A few people told me they could see me doing real estate. So on that winter day in my kitchen, I found a course not too far away. My parents offered to watch my daughter for the two weekends, and my mom even offered to pay for class for me as a gift. I've always believed that when I get "green lights and open doors" I know I'm on the right path. The whole time, from idea to completion, these green lights and open doors eased my way. I studied relentlessly before my test and passed it. Now it's been three years, and it all started that one day when I took that one idea and moved toward it through an outside action. It's easy to think an idea is just an idea, but it's not. It's a pregnant creation. Everything you've done up till now, you've taken from a seed, which is invisible (a thought), to a full outward experience. This is why your thoughts are so powerful.

Everything comes to you through an idea. The idea may have come from the Universe...every idea had a place of origin in the ethers. As a creator, you take the idea and act on it. Sometimes we have these great ideas and leave them alone to starve and finally die off from our consciousness.

Instead of dismissing the ideas that cross your mind, what if you stopped to feed these creative seeds instead? What if you gave them life through your actions? What if you choose to protect these sprouts and watched them grow into oak tree–sized dreams?

You can prevent your dreams from getting lost and leaving through constant care and attention. It comes down to putting your faith, hope, and love into them. Every idea inside of you that makes you feel alive is a seed. It will either grow into whatever size container you can imagine, or it will wither away and die. What you do with these seeds is what will determine the quality of your life.

Don't wait for things to be perfect to start toward your dreams. There is no better time than now. You don't know how long you have. Live your life to the fullest and never stop pursuing being all that you can be!

3. Believe that You Can

Believing in what you can or can't do determines what you will or won't do. Just as a thought precedes action, belief precedes experience. The unseen, formless substance of consciousness from which everything derives is directed into form and experience by the orders it takes from your beliefs. This is why it's so important to believe in yourself if you want to change your life!

The challenge arises when you don't believe you can be, do, or have something. This is an area I'm very familiar with and continue to work on. Whenever you're looking to improve your life, your old ego stories will rear their ugly heads in an attempt to keep you small, because that's where you've had your beliefs set for so long. There is a way out!

It's been said many times that repetition is the mother of skill. I couldn't agree more, especially when it comes to reconditioning your beliefs. You may have believed you couldn't do better, have better, or be better for years. I'm here to tell you that's a lie. You can! *If* you commit to working on yourself every day, you can overcome the lies you've told yourself! As boring as it sounds, it happens through daily practice. The key is to find ways to bring your focus back throughout the day to what the best you feels like.

When I'm meditating in the morning, it's easy to get my Zen on. But then the day gets going and a challenge hits and bam! All of a sudden, that Zen place is nowhere to be found. Can you relate? Index cards have proven very useful to bring my focus back to what I'm trying to create in my belief system. After meditation, I'll get a hit of inspiration or a mantra. Some people call them affirmations. For me, it's anything that will help me to focus during the day. It usually starts with, "I'm so grateful…" and then I write something to support my new belief on an index card. Some examples are:

> "I'm so grateful to know I'm worthy and deserving of the very best life has to offer, and I lovingly allow myself to accept it now."

> "I'm so grateful to be creating a strong, beautiful, and abundant relationship with money!"

> "I'm so grateful to be creating a life of love, peace, prosperity, health, fun, opportunity, and endless adventure!"

Writing out statements that support your new beliefs is a powerful way of creating your new beliefs. During the day, look at them often and think about how experiencing these things makes you feel. Looking at them *often* is the secret. We can have a very short attention span. It takes willingness and consistency, but you will be amazed at how you begin to think differently. The roots will grow with repetition, and when you don't quit, these thoughts will become your new beliefs! As you make this a habit, you see experiences unfold to match these beliefs. Someday you will look back and need a telescope to see who that person was before.

4. One Thing at a Time

Learning to focus on one thing at a time is the way to reach your goals. Unfortunately, this goes against the multi-tasking epidemic in our current society. The truth is, when making changes in your life, less is more. When you focus on one thing at a time, you're going to advance quicker than if you spread your energy in many different directions. Personally, I've learned to focus on one area at a time. Right now, it's been this book. Once this project is complete, I've got others lined up that I'll do the same thing with. Finding an extra one or two hours a day to focus on just one thing grows like compound interest. Before you know it, you'll make steady progress and reach your goals.

Focusing on one thing at a time can be used to improve relationships, grow your business, improve your health, clean your home, start a new project, learn how to be financially sound, pay off debt, or anything.

I used to try to do too many things at once and never make measurable progress in any one area. After reading *The One Thing*, by Gary Keller, I committed to *my one thing*. It took so much pressure off me trying to do *everything*. I will say that at first, I felt like I was letting other parts of my life down. *Why couldn't I be superwoman?* Although I began making great progress in one area, others suffered. I felt guilty, until I realized that not all areas are created equal. It's OK for life to feel a little unbalanced when you're breaking new ground to improve yourself. Especially since I was making such strides in the areas that mattered most to me, I decided to let go of unrealistic expectations. I made only the most important things non-negotiable and accepted that not everything made this list.

One easy way to stay focused is to use your phone's timer and the do not disturb button. It's simple and it works! I do this for writing, reading, meditating, journaling, planning, creating vision books, working out, marketing, and even for walking with my dog. Having blocks of time devoted to anything that's important means it gets a piece of my undivided attention. I have whole days blocked off for quality time with my daughter. It comes down to making what matters most a regular part of your life. Your time will soon begin to look different than before you time-blocked. It becomes more intentional when you take stock of your time and use it to create a great life on purpose.

5. Be Willing to Go Big

I believe it's just as easy to go big as it is to go small. Both require effort and both involve discomfort, obstacles, and setbacks. The difference is in the outcome. To go big is to own your deepest goals and desires. It may seem far away from where you now stand, but so does everything at first. Everyone who has ever achieved great things had to go where they've never gone before. It requires believing in something bigger and better. It stretches you. Going big is beautiful because it requires you to truly live outside your comfort zone. The best part is who you become in the process. Watching all the small victories as your life evolves gives you a satisfaction that you can't buy anywhere. Learning what a powerful creator you are is when the light of who you really are begins to shine.

The other day I listened to a Lewis Howe School of Greatness podcast called *Become a Superhuman and Achieve The Impossible with Iron Cowboy James Lawrence*. This man ran fifty Ironman triathlons in fifty days in fifty states. I highly recommend listening to it. Hearing his story made me admire the remarkable strength and endurance of the human spirit. It's an amazing example of using our mental potential to accomplish what's never been done before.

Maybe you will never want to do a triathlon, but whatever going big means for you will require you to set sails in a direction you've never gone before. Going big is never accomplished by sticking with what you already know and have done. Once you make up your mind to go big, you must learn how to train it to command your physical actions, thoughts, and decisions. Practice living this way, and you will find new strength. Every successful person must learn that your mind controls your life. When you're no longer willing to settle for less, the opportunity for realizing your mind's true capacity is at its greatest. Many people live mediocre lives and, at the end, look back with regret. This never needs to happen to you. If you're reading this book, your soul and spirit probably crave more. This craving is a beautiful gift. Use it to head in a new, better direction. Use it to start seeing *how you can* instead of *why you can't*.

Be willing to go big.

WRAP UP

It takes courage to make a change, but remember that you're worth the investment. You can always reevaluate what really works and doesn't work. You are constantly evolving. By embracing life's changes, you can enjoy transforming your life into what would make you feel most fulfilled and satisfied. Remember this is YOUR life and YOU are responsible for your happiness.

My friend Gillian once told me that in life there are many chapters and it's OK to change and define what is right for you. What felt right for you when you were ten is different than what is right at twenty, thirty, forty, fifty, sixty, seventy...or one hundred! You must define what the best version of you is NOW.

LESSON I ASSIGNMENT

1. List three supportive/affirming statements about what you're grateful for, in the life you're creating now:

    1. _____

       _____

    2. _____

       _____

    3. _____

       _____

2. List three examples of one thing that you can start doing today, regardless of things not being perfect?

    1. _____

       _____

       _____

    2. _____

       _____

    3. _____

       _____

       _____

3. Write down three ways that you're willing to go big now!

    1. _____

       _____

    2. _____

       _____

    3. _____

       _____

       _____

2 THE LESSON OF INTENTION

A man is literally what he thinks, his character being the complete sum of all his thoughts.

—James Allen

Once upon a time—even before my daughter was born—I sat in serious doubt as to what I wanted in my life. We're not talking about a little uncertainty here and there; it was more like I simply couldn't make up my mind about *many* things. Call it indecision, fear, lack of clarity, or whatever you'd like, but I knew it was a stumbling block to living a satisfying life. Over time, this really started bothering me, which led me to analyze my life from a more introspective view.

One afternoon, while sitting on a rock next to a river and watching my dog, go in and out of the water, enjoying how it felt to be there, I felt quiet inside and began thinking about why I couldn't seem to make up my mind on so many things. At first I thought that maybe I liked to keep my options open and therefore didn't like to commit, but the more I allowed myself to *feel* the truth beneath the surface, I could sense an element of fear. There were also feelings of being undeserving and not worthy of aiming too high in particular areas. The worst part was doubting that I even *could* experience success in some particular areas. This was my ugly truth, the root of feeling like a deer in the headlights when making decisions: fear and self-doubt.

I knew being honest with myself was the only way to find the answers I was looking for. To get the answers to an inside problem, I had to go to a place I wasn't sure I could come back from. *Going within takes courage.*

Finding a solution led me to uncover the beliefs I carried. Once I discovered the beliefs I could then see the stories I'd attached to them. These stories had no truth, but my belief in them made them *my truth*. This in turn altered how high I had set the bar for myself on what was or wasn't possible for my life. Once I submitted to a belief, the stories surrounding it showed up as supporting evidence. I told myself that I could never be/do/have this or that, because *I believed* that was only for *other* people. After fueling this belief with the story that "other people were basically better than me in some way, success being the evidence," I became unable to vibrate at a higher frequency than this belief allowed. In turn, only that which vibrated at this low frequency was able to make its way into my experience. This set me up to continuously reinforce my belief through the stories I carried around that reinforced a cycle which began, and ran strong, for many years.

Basically, the events in your life that don't feel good, but keep showing up, point to a limiting belief and the stories around it. Realizing there is no one else who was going to solve my problems, that these were my creations to begin with, gave me a chance to change the one thing that I could control: myself.

My intention was—and still is to this day—to become the best version of myself I can. While I've had a lot of personal challenges, I've also experienced many ah-ha moments. One thing that has become crystal clear is how important it is to know your intention. We don't need to wait until the end of our lives to realize how precious our time is. We can begin setting new intentions for a better quality of life right here and now. You can set the sails for new chapters in the story of your life that *you* get to create, and it begins with setting new intentions.

Merriam-Webster's dictionary defines intention as "what one intends to do, or bring about." Planning with intention is like having directions to where you're going.

My intention was to be free of limiting beliefs and intentionally create a life I love! This changed my life in so many ways. I learned to say yes when I meant it, and that no is also a complete sentence. Giving life my all shifted how I allocated my time, big time! I realized that how I spent my time was precisely related to the progress I either made...or didn't. Finally, a decision that turned out to be a real game-changer was that I decided to spend a portion of every day on personal development. Creating habits that reinforced my personal development felt so good that they took hold of me in a strong way and continue today.

Waking up early to exercise made me realize that it's possible to change yourself physically, mentally, and energetically. It made a huge difference in my confidence. This was about wanting to *feel good unapologetically.* Understanding that repetition is the mother of skill, I learned to feed myself steady doses of mental nutrition through reading books and listening to YouTube videos that inspired, taught me something, and raised my vibration by association. What I mean by *vibration* here is that when you feel good, you vibrate at a higher frequency and attract more of what feels good. Likewise, when you feel bad, you vibrate at a much lower frequency and attract more of what feels bad.

There were even a couple friendships that ended because our energies were no longer aligned. Changes took place in my work when I realized that happiness and living in a balanced way is priceless to my inner landscape, and there is no dollar amount that can buy that. Overall, my intention to become the best version of myself became the driving force that led me to question everything I thought I knew.

FIVE QUESTIONS TO IDENTIFY
A LACK OF INTENTION

1. Do you feel stuck and confused in an area of your life?

2. Do you want to feel better but don't know where to begin?

3. Have you found yourself wondering why others seemed to have figured this out and you don't know why you haven't?

4. Are you sick and tired of complaining about the same situation?

5. Do you feel you're not living the best version of yourself?

If you answered YES to any of these questions, you're not alone—but you're also not doomed to continue living this way if you're willing to change. Setting an intention to begin living as the best version yourself simply requires being open to seeing things differently and changing your perception.

Changing perception is often overlooked because it's invisible, internal work. As human beings, we all have the ability to choose our thoughts. Which thoughts we choose become the determining factor in our lives. The ability to use this powerful tool is part of your birthright as a creative being. Although this often isn't taught in schools, nor talked about at home, perception *IS* a huge factor in the level of satisfaction you'll experience. Our beliefs determine the lens through which we see the world. This lens keeps us in a proportionately sized container in terms of what we can do, be, and have. To question and analyze what drives your whole life is essential in order to realize your greatest potential.

FIVE METHODS TO CREATE A NEW INTENTION

1. Ask Different Questions:

We get what we focus on. Unfortunately, it's very easy to become distracted in our fast-paced world. Oftentimes, we don't even know what our intention is. We get swamped with so many tasks that we don't ask what we want out of life. The key to remember is that you are either leading your life, or it's happening by default.

Focusing on what you don't like even if it's your current reality is unfortunately exactly what keeps you stuck. To begin changing your focus, try asking different questions. Instead of focusing on what you don't want, ask what you DO want.

Below are some questions that can help you refocus your thoughts. It's helpful to sit quietly and, after each question, close your eyes and allow your heart and intuition to answer honestly. By placing one hand over your heart and one over your solar plexus, you can invite your truth to come forth.

- How would living as the best version of you FEEL?
- If you woke up in the morning as the best version of you, what would you do first?
- If you could live anywhere, where would the best version of you live and why?
- Why would feeling more confident being the best version of you be more fun?
- How would doing one thing every day toward becoming the best version of you change your life?
- Would the best version of you look differently in some way? The way you dress, carry you, speak, etc. If so, what can you do today to move closer to this version of you?

These questions will make it easy to compare and contrast your best version with your current reality. Some people say they have no choice, but you always have a choice to change your mind. Even things that don't feel particularly great have value. They are what make you strong, allow you to appreciate when you do feel good, and offer opportunities of growth. It's not always easy to change, but it's harder being unhappy and feeling like a victim. The choice is always yours. I've learned to say thank you to my challenges because, on the other side of every challenge, there's always an upgrade and leveling up in terms of personal growth.

When asking these questions, you can train your mind to come up with different answers. When you answer a question from the perspective of the best version of you, it alters your response and creates space to see other options. If you can practice answering these questions daily, over time your responses will go from feeling very unfamiliar to feeling more familiar, then very familiar, and finally they will become natural.

DAILY PRACTICE is critical! In order to get good at anything, it must be done until it feels natural. I'm not going to lie...renewing your mind and your beliefs is not for the weak of heart. It's going to take some time.

But *if* you persist, you'll be able to truly experience an intentionally satisfying life.

2. Borrow Energy by Association

There is an energy behind every person/place/thing/idea/thought. What's around us affects our energy whether we realize it or not. One of my favorite methods to change my intention is to change my associations. I like to find mentors who inspire my thinking. There are so many different types of mentors out there today—you don't need to even know your mentor personally. Your mentor can be an author or speaker. You can read their books in the evenings or listen to them on YouTube every morning while getting ready for the day. Simply by associating yourself with them, your energy is raised to a higher frequency. Your intention to live the best version of yourself becomes stronger when you absorb the energy of others who are like-minded in their intentions.

Whatever it is you see or think in terms of becoming the best version of yourself, something already exists at that exact energetic frequency. Your best version could include a place you'd love to live, clothes you'd love to wear, a vacation you've dreamed of taking, being in love, living in a healthy body, doing work you love, or anything else that fits into the best version of you. For example, if it's a place to live, find out as much as you can about that place, check out real estate there and spend a day driving around and checking out the sights. If you imagine dressing in beautiful clothes, go try them on and experience the feeling of wearing them! If you want to be in love, start by doing the very things you'd do if you were already in love—like upgrading your underwear and bed sheets... just doing this can seriously upgrade your energy! If living in a healthy body is something you're moving toward, start shopping at Whole Foods, sign up for an exercise class, and join a local gym or walking club. If the best version of you is doing work that you love, learn more about the jobs you're passionate about. Even better, find someone who's already doing it and reach out to them! Ask how they got into it. If they're local, offer to buy them coffee or a lunch. I've found that people are very willing to share their experience with you *when you ask*!

Your goal is to be around whatever inspires you as much as possible. Repeated exposure will create an intention within yourself. You'll begin to realize that if someone else can do it, YOU can do it too!

3. Get an Accountability Partner

This part of creating a new intention can be hard, but if you want to get serious about becoming the best version of yourself, getting an accountability partner makes it real. Many people would never share their inner intentions, because it means someone else is paying attention to your progress. However, if you share your intention, you're more likely to follow through because of this very same fact. For example, while writing this book, I met with my book coach every week to go over my progress. Before I did this, my book was stuck *in my head!* You need to get things out of your head and into reality.

Having an accountability partner can be exciting because once you start making consistent progress, it will bring you greater satisfaction. You get hooked on seeing the possibilities and stretching outside your comfort zone. A comfort zone sounds nice until you realize it doesn't push you to become the best version of yourself. When you're uncomfortable, you know you're growing and changing. Being uncomfortable is *necessary and OK!* Coaching clients tell me all the time that because we have an appointment, they show up. It's because they show up that they get results.

Your accountability partner can be someone you know or just someone who is willing to check in with you periodically. Ideally, your accountability partner will be someone who has mastered the area in which you're to be held accountable. If you're looking to improve your relationship with your spouse, you don't want to pick someone who's in an unhealthy relationship themselves.

There are lots of ways to find an accountability partner. You can research the topic in Meetups or google. Or find a local group working on the area you'd like to improve. Network with people and ask if they know anyone with expertise you could reach out to. Remember that the energy of your accountability partner will affect you, so it's a good idea to pick someone who is supportive, caring, and who you respect and feel safe to share openly with.

4. Create a Vision Board or Book

Pictures, phrases, and physical items are powerful stimulators for your intention! Some people create a vision board with Pinterest, but personally I think the experience is stronger when you can actually *feel* the physical components of your vision board or book. To create a vision board, simply collect pictures, phrases, or items that make you excited and support your idea of the best version of you! Before this book was even completed, I had the cover designed and put it in my vision book. Seeing my book cover energized me to finish the book!

Whatever it is for you, have fun with it and let your imagination explore! Go through magazines and Web sites. Print out anything from the Internet that calls to you. If you're tech savvy, try using Photoshop to make cool images! The important part is to make it a habit by reviewing it daily. Reconditioning your mind to reinforce your intention and live the best version of you *always* requires repetition.

5. Write it Down!

Another method to creating a new intention is to write it down. There is something that happens when you take what's in your head and write it down. I usually write down an intention as if it has already happened. The important part is to be as specific as possible.

Vague: *To complete my book.*

Clear: *I'm so happy and excited to be holding my book and be a published author!*

When I write my intention, I also write down the feelings I will experience when I achieve my goal. I use words such as *excited, confident, thankful, happy, awesome, game-changer, loving life, upgraded, leveled-up, inspired, motivated, energetic,* etc. These words stimulate emotion because they give you a chance to identify how reaching your intention/goal *will make you feel* once you've achieved it. You might find that it's not the goal itself that motivates you, but rather who you become, how your life will change, and how you will feel!

Write each separate intention on its own index card and go over each one daily. If you look over them once every hour, it will keep these intentions front and center.

As you practice this, close your eyes and jump into the picture. Live out your intention in your mind. Be the person NOW who has already achieved your intention! Experiencing the excitement and gratitude of achieving your intention begins to shift your vibration more toward it. Daily practice will make you realize that how you feel begins in your mind. When you allow yourself to truly feel how delicious it is to achieve and become the best version of yourself, you'll begin to see that you are indeed a creator.

WRAP UP

Having an intention for a specific outcome must come from ***within you.*** To truly change your life, you need to start with YOU. There have been so many times that I felt stuck in certain areas—and it felt terrible!! The crazy thing is that, as terrible as I felt, I still didn't take action to change it.

The intention to become the best person you can be develops inner strength. This kind of strength says that, no matter what happens, you will learn from it, grow from it, become smarter for it, and add more value for having gone through it. Viewing life this way sets you up for success because it doesn't rely on anything external. It is the one part of life that is truly yours to own. Owning this kind of intention is owning your power.

To experience life differently means that you're going to need to upgrade and level up your game. To experience differently, you must become different. This may come in the form of new skills to learn, new people to associate with, investing your time reading books on the subject, attending seminars, getting a coach, or enrolling in a course. It could mean not doing certain things, too, like not buying junk food, hanging with pity-party people, or wasting hours on social media. No matter what area you're intending to improve, you need to start with who you need to become.

I'll give you an example. There was a time I experienced a ton of pain in the area of cash flow. It either flowed, or the faucet shut off completely.

When I became fearful about money, I'd freak myself out and imagine all of the worst things that could happen!! Of course this spiraled into depression and isolation. Feeling paralyzed inside, I was constantly tired, which as a single mom with a business to run was not cool! I realized that ***I needed to change my state of mind in order to feel differently.***

My intention was to feel good while learning new skills around and about money. This included increasing the value I was able to give to others and understanding that money was simply a value exchange for what we give.

This launched a very strong chain of events. One of the things I did was take an inventory of my talents and things I was already offering to clients that I could expand on. I've always loved to write, but the big F (fear) always got in my way. My intention was so clear, though, that I started slamming my fist down when that old negative voice showed up. I wrote down my goal to publish a book as a way to give more back. This opened up a whole bunch of new challenges, like learning the publishing process, carving the time to type it out, creating an outline, finding the right designer to help create the cover and interior design, finding the right editor, and so on. The steps seemed endless, and it was all so new that I felt like a kindergartener in this new adventure. It gave me a sense of how challenging it can be to change and sometimes it felt like my brain hurt! Before long, however, I began to gravitate toward successful people who had already written and published books. I wanted to learn what I didn't know!

One day, a friend texted me that they were running a BOGO special for tickets to a Success and Wealth Summit right in Boston, near where I live (once again, notice that you attract what you focus on). So I signed up for an event on success and wealth featuring Bethenny Frankel, Marcus Lemonis, Tony Robbins, Tom Brady, and Julian Edelmen, to name a few. I was so pumped! Talk about a different level of energy! This was exactly what I needed, and I began to see how I could not only change my state by making different choices but I could change my life! My motivation kicked up a notch, and I began reading books and listening to anything that inspired a state of abundance and success.

There was a relentless hunger inside me to succeed and never return to my fear-based mentality regarding money. My relationship with money needed to change, and getting honest was the first step. On a physical level, I also did things to stimulate my energy and vibration. Things like exercising every day, eating clean, taking lots of walks in nature, staying hydrated, getting enough sleep, and taking serious time for self-care each and every day.

It all comes down to taking the time to really look into your life, see what's not working, get honest about it, and then set your intention. *Your intention is your ideal outcome.* It's the big picture; the action steps are the details. Your intention will pull you through when a to-do list won't. Intention triumphs these kinds of lists because *it goes down deep to your soul and how that makes you feel.* Having emotions backing your intentions makes you an unstoppable force in a language that the Universe speaks.

LESSON 2 ASSIGNMENT

To begin identifying the best version of yourself, sit down and focus on the following nine areas. *Ask yourself what you want to do, have, and be in these areas of your life.* Notice what comes up. If there are some improvements you'd like to make, *write out your new intentions right below that area.* Congratulate yourself for getting honest!

Personal growth

> *Intentions:* _____

> _____

Relationships

> *Intentions:* _____

> _____

Health

> *Intentions:* _____

> _____

Love

   Intentions: _____

   _____

Spirituality

   Intentions: _____

   _____

Finances

   Intentions: _____

   _____

Home Environment

   Intentions: _____

   _____

Social Life

   Intentions: _____

   _____

Confidence

   Intentions: _____

   _____

3 THE LESSON OF
MOVING FORWARD

It's not what happens in the world that determines the major part of
your future. What happens, happens to us all. The key is what you do
about it.

—Jim Rohn

I was once in a relationship that was dysfunctional in so many ways but
also incredibly difficult for me to get out of. Despite knowing it was pulling me away from living as the best version of myself, I felt addicted to
the drama. Long after my intuition told me it wasn't healthy, the relationship just kept dragging on and on because I made no effort to change it.
Eventually, I got worn out and couldn't deny the fact that it was time to
move on with my life.

Ever notice that knowing something in your head yet feeling the pain
of it in your heart creates a sort of internal tug of war? I remember taking
many long walks and asking the Universe for wisdom, discernment, and
strength to guide me along this rocky chapter. As usual, when you ask, an
idea comes. The idea was my *awareness* that *before this relationship, I
was OK*. It felt monumental to simply acknowledge that there was a time,

before I even knew this person, that I was really, truly OK. Although it didn't feel like it at that time, I knew I'd get back to me if I moved forward and gave myself time.

Truth be told, it did take quite some time. Over the coming days and months of continually being willing, open, and disciplined enough to care about myself, the day did arrive where I had myself back. The turning point came when I stopped looking back to what was and kept my eyes on what lay ahead. This isn't easy to do because, once again, it's uncomfortable to get out of our comfort zone. However, in order to improve our lives, it's an inevitable fact that you will have to at some point, or you will stay stuck. You might feel bad or like you're betraying someone by leaving a situation that isn't good for your life, but it's worse to be held back out of fear. You'll regret never giving your all for the rest of your life.

I'm glad to say that, as hard as ending certain chapters of your life can be, there are many more ahead that can make you happier than you ever thought possible. Be willing to be messy in life when your intuition leads you in another direction. There is a reason you feel pulled to grow and leave chapters you've outgrown. It's to be the best person you can be. Let your light shine!

Merriam-Webster's dictionary defines movement as "marked by or capable of movement."

Merriam-Webster's dictionary defines forward as "moving, tending, or leading toward a position in front" and also, "of, relating to, or getting ready for the future."

You are capable of **movement** in your life. Your mind goes where you direct it, through the thoughts you choose to think. If you truly own your mental potential, you will never stay stuck in any situation. This is the first fact in moving forward.

The second ingredient needed for movement is to consider where your movement is going. Sometimes we move in a backward or even circular motion. Over time, this leads us to feel dissatisfied because we aren't growing. Just as our eyes look forward and not backward, looking ahead and making forward movement is one of the powerful ways to improve your life.

Let me be perfectly clear. You cannot recreate the past, so why focus there? Right here, right now you have work to do. It has to do with how you will move forward. Some people exude a kind of swagger that lets you know they're in charge of where they're going. You can tell because of how they carry themselves. They have an inner confidence. They're moving forward in life with this confidence. I'll tell you the great secret about confident people: *they made the choice to be.*

Years ago, I learned a valuable lesson when I used to sell Mary Kay. My sales director told our team something one time that I still use to this day. She told us to pretend that Mary Kay herself was standing at our door and to never leave the house unless we looked our best and had our "face" on. We were selling the product, so it only made sense to wear and present it well. What was interesting to me was that when I took extra effort, I really did feel better and more confident. I believe this confidence had a direct influence on my success with my business.

The energy we give off in the way we present ourselves to the world determines what we will attract. Most of us have had days where we'd rather stay in bed and not deal with whatever is going on in our lives, but this is the *exact time* your extra effort is most effective. It works because you're choosing how you're *going to be vs. how you feel.*

There are plenty of days that moving forward won't necessarily make you feel awesome, because our emotions can be influenced by so many things. But remember that you can still choose to show up as the best version of yourself *despite how you feel*. Over time, you'll realize that you can choose to feel good even on the days you may have responded differently before.

Little things can make a difference in how you feel about yourself and in your confidence. Iron your clothes, smell good, get your nails and toes done, dye your hair or buy a wig, get new bras and underwear, get rid of clothes that make you feel dull and tired, stand tall with your eyes up and your posture straight, smile and make the most out of this day you were given. Learn to be thankful. Over time, any little change you can make in the direction of being the best version of yourself will grow like compound interest. All things start with a thought and a small beginning. Be thankful for every small effort you make toward your self-improvement. It's just one day at a time, trying to live your life to the best of your ability.

FIVE QUESTIONS TO HELP IDENTIFY IF YOU'RE NOT MOVING FORWARD

1. Do you repeat the past every day…even telling it to anyone else who will listen?
2. Do you frequently feel like your life is not where you thought it would be…and feel stuck?
3. Do you wish you had more confidence?
4. Are you bored and unsatisfied?
5. Are you a control freak and consumed with everything being perfect *before* you begin moving forward?

The kind of choices I'm talking about are the kind that you AREN'T making, not the ones you make that turn out badly. It's normal to sometimes screw up a business or relationship or get into financial trouble that you learn from and make better choices moving forward. You learn valuable life lessons from each and every experience.

Many times, I've had to get honest and really look at how I was moving forward in certain areas…or NOT moving forward. You can't change what you don't acknowledge that is causing you to settle, not care, rely on addictions, or a slew of other issues. You can recognize these areas because they feel like stuck energy, which zaps your life force. Since energy is life, over time this can have a detrimental effect on your outlook and quality of life. The time to act on improving your life is now!

The good news is that there is a better way. You can move forward with a style that your confidence and whole life will grow from. It begins inside of yourself. It takes some practice but is well worth it.

FIVE METHODS TO MOVE FORWARD

1. Decide to Let Go of the Past

Whatever the past has been for you, it has brought you to this very moment. While there may have been some things you'd prefer were different, it's important to realize that when you focus your energy on what is behind you, you are not able to move forward. To become the best version of yourself, you'll need to let go of the past. This can be a challenge, but one method that can help you let go is writing your past a letter. It's a way to honor it for the lessons it's contained. You can use your past as a beautiful contrast for the kind of life you're going to create in the future.

Use every experience to your advantage by asking questions such as:

- What did I learn?
- How did I grow?
- What do I know I want to be/do/have NOW, because of what I've experienced?
- What do I value more NOW because of this experience?
- How has this made me a better person?

Asking questions like these shifts your energy to focus on what you've GAINED. It's easy to forget, but it gets easier the more you practice it. As creatures of habit, we sometimes forget...until it becomes so important that we don't. Sometimes the places that brought you the most pain turn out to be the most fertile ground for the best you to emerge. Pain gives us perspective, contrast, and teaches us why we want to do/be/have better. Embrace what's been in your life, instead of feeling that it's made you unworthy or undeserving of a great life. Your belief in the meaning you give your past is what moves you forward or keeps you stuck in it.

When you do feel stuck, there are still ways to help yourself move forward. When uncertainty or fear rears its ugly head, there's a visualization that has often helped me get me back on track. Sit quietly and just let your mind go to the last day of your life for a few moments. Here you are, on your last day, and getting the chance to look over your life and how you've lived it and how you felt about yourself. Are you satisfied with how you've lived? What do you regret not doing? What do you wish you could do differently?

This exercise is a great way to gain perspective. It can be a great way to learn not to sweat the small stuff and get going with what's meaningful.

When you see that your life is brief, and your job is to share your gifts and contribute in the way only YOU can, it shifts your focus. You begin to ask: ***"What am I waiting for?"***

Earlier today, I visited a place close to where I used to live. It's a beautiful park where I walked my dog for years. There was a huge weeping birch tree in the middle that looked so grand it reminded me of the tree in the movie *Avatar*. Today when I walked through the park, I felt sad to see that the tree was dying. It made me think of how life is, how there is a rising and falling with all of life. It also made me realize there are times in life to be and do certain things. Looking at your life from the end of it can really create perspective on what really matters. The truth of our lives is that there IS a day you will *get out of the car*. If you can remember this, it will help you defeat fear and do that thing that's in your heart.

Thinking from the end can also give you clarity when you ask the following questions:

- What gifts do I have to share with the world?
- What can I give that will add value to others?
- What legacy do I want to leave behind?
- What dream, yearning, or calling still lives and wants to be expressed?
- Are my doubts and fears worth the price of what I will miss out on if I don't live full out?

Remember that no one ever has been served well by playing small. Have faith that you have a purpose, and only you can fill the role you're meant to play in the world. Your life and the quality of your fulfillment are largely determined by the kind of thoughts you allow to consume your focus.

To change your thoughts, you need to change your patterns by deliberately choosing that you will not settle for less than the best thoughts.

Notice your thoughts. The thoughts you believe are true carry powerful intentions. When you notice a thought that makes you feel icky, you can simply choose to not receive it. You can literally say to any thought, either from yourself or another, that is disempowering, *"I don't receive that."*

This practice takes patience and persistence, but the rewards you'll reap from mastering your thoughts are simply immeasurable.

2. Clear Your Mind

When your head's full of noise and craziness, it's challenging to move forward in a meaningful way. There are many methods to clear your mind. I've found a few helpful tricks.

One is to take out a blank piece of paper and draw a box. Inside the box, write down everything that's pressing on your mind. Things like your to-do list, something that you may not have an answer to, errands, calls to make, work-related things, projects, things that are bothering you, something that happened that hasn't been resolved and is taking up space and energy…literally anything that's distracting you. Putting things on paper gives you a different perspective.

Next write, *"Universe please guide, inspire, and grant me wisdom with all of these. Thank you."* We often don't feel supported and get the help we need because we forget to ask. Saying "Thank you" implies that you acknowledge that not only does the Universe hear you, but the guidance, inspiration, and wisdom is on its way. Have faith that when you ask, you shall receive. Another good way to ask for guidance is by using the Serenity Prayer: *"God, grant me the serenity to accept the things I cannot change, the courage to change the things I can, and the wisdom to know the difference."*

Next, write all of the feelings you'd like to *feel* today below the box. I often find myself write down things like peace, joy, love, fun, flow, balance, green lights, open doors, abundance, prosperity, strong, confident, growing, awesome, inspired, excited, synchronicity, and beautiful. As you write down the feelings you'd like to feel today, you're actually sending a powerful signal out to the Universe because you're calling out your intentions in a clear, specific way. You can have a busy schedule, and a lot on your mind, and still choose to be aligned with how you want to feel in your day.

Once you write down how you want to feel, look back at what you wrote in the box and ask how you can incorporate these feelings into what you wrote. For example, if you wrote that you'd like to feel fun, look and see where you can have more fun with everything you do today. Laugh more, smile more, be the person who enjoys having fun! Often, knowing how you want to feel will make it apparent which items in the box are really important right now, as opposed to the ones you don't need to concern your mind and energy today.

This is about clearing space in your mind. Realize that you must be intentional in your day, but having a hundred things on your mind doesn't feel good. It's not surprising if this exercise highlights the contrast between how you want to feel and what you actually feel. Many things are better delegated if possible, or you can let them go. Much of what we think can be unproductive. The act of writing it down gives you a chance to see the exact ingredients that are going to create how you feel. Again, this gives you choices.

Another way to clear your mind is to get out into nature every day. Getting out where you can breathe fresh air, walk, and see beautiful views can do wonders in clearing your mind. Nature's healing and soothing effects can help when your mind's congested. Take time to just be. Leave your phone for a few hours, or at least put it on do not disturb.

Lastly, there's sleep. When you're constantly exhausted from not getting enough sleep, it can seem impossible to clear your mind. While many people have gotten used to barely getting enough rest, sleep is our body's way to restore and heal. Over time, you may begin to think that how you feel is just how you are, when you may simply be exhausted. Lack of sleep can lead to confusion, overwhelm, negativity, overeating, and other symptoms that will interfere with moving forward. If this feels like you, become proactive and look for ways to get in some more ZZZZs. Even a powernap for a half-hour in the afternoon can boost your energy level.

3. Finish your day/week before you start it.

This was really a game-changer in how I was able to manage my time and energy. It's kind of like planning your time backward. When I know I want to work out to feel great and stay healthy, I mark all my workouts for the week on a calendar. I also mark out time for my clients, classes, talks, meal prep, time with my daughter, time for the market and errands, walks with my dog, date night, get-togethers with friends, personal development time such as studying/practicing/learning new skills, and pretty much *any other thing that's important to make happen.* Marking out time in my schedule for these things means they *will* happen.

Every Sunday, looking at the upcoming week gives me a chance to realistically decide what else, *if anything*, I'd say yes to during the week. Years ago, when I didn't use this method to move forward, time would have any which way with me. My mind would get hooked into anything that got my attention. Unfortunately, days, months, and years went by with little progress.

When you don't plan, anything can grab your precious focus and energy. This creates a cycle of never getting the things done you thought you would. Anything that steals your focus ought to be analyzed. If something or someone continuously wastes your time and energy, minimize your exposure to that thing or eliminate it completely. I'm all for free thought during meditation, walks in nature, and having fun with the people you love, BUT when it comes to life's time and energy, I'm not so generous if it moves me in the opposite direction of being the best version of myself. This isn't selfish—it's a successful habit that will move you toward a satisfying life.

You simply can't do it all. Trying to do everything, and please everyone, will leave you energetically bankrupt. Learning to kindly say no is actually saying yes to what matters most to you: a fulfilling life, being the best version of yourself.

Healthy boundaries and limits regarding your time and energy can be efficiently handled by planning your week ahead. Of course life happens, and some things you can't plan for. Adjustments must be made. When this happens, you can look to see if you can reschedule vital things.

For the most part, sticking to a schedule that's aligned with your goals actually *frees up your mind* because you know what you're doing and when. Within structure there is freedom. I find it to be a rather comforting feeling, knowing that space has been made for all important parts of my life. If I fail to plan and drop the ball by not reaching my goals, there's no one else to blame but myself. Taking 100 percent responsibility for how your life turns out may mean putting more effort out than perhaps you previously have. The effort you put in to planning your week will lessen over time. You'll also get the satisfaction of checking things off as you do them, seeing the progress you're making every day.

If you're a visual person like I am, you can also highlight your calendar in different colors. For me, yellow is for work and clients, blue is for appointments, green is for money-making activities such as marketing, pink is for all of the things I do for self-care and spending time with the people I love (workouts, massage, time with my daughter, friends, etc.), purple is for appointments for personal development like reading, and orange is for real estate stuff. The bottom line is to make it work whatever way suits you. Getting into a routine of planning ahead allows you to see exactly how you're spending your time.

4. Decide to enjoy the journey.

Make the conscious decision to enjoy each step in your journey! This will help change the feelings of drudgery (let's be honest) that may crop up when you see how far you may be from where you intend to be/do/have. Deciding to make your journey an enjoyable one means asking yourself every day: *"What can I do today to feel good?"* It can be anything! Sign up for that course you've been dying to take, ask that person out on a date, buy yourself or someone you love flowers, make plans with a friend, schedule a massage, take a nap, or whatever you want to do to feel good.

I try to spend time every day focusing on things that make me feel joy. This practice can literally change your life. Remembering joy—even if you're not feeling it right now—switches your vibration. With daily practice, you can become more comfortable living in joy. Staying *in joy*, will allow you to *enjoy* your life.

Besides being good for your health, as you move forward in joy it will become clearer what actually does and doesn't bring you joy (huge hint to what you may want to focus on!). It may be time to do some housecleaning, as joy will bring you clarity on what is and isn't working in your life. Remember, life is always forward, and being able to move forward despite fear takes courage. You can make this much easier if you focus on feeling joy, because joy is a part of your true nature. You've heard the saying, "The truth will set you free," and the one who wants to be free is YOU!

Joy can't be faked, which is why it's a fabulous place to start focusing on what you want.

You are never alone in this journey. The Universe supports you and wants you to be happy, joyful, successful, loved, abundant, and free to be the best version of you! There are no awards for *sacrificing* your joy for someone or something because you were made to feel you **should**. I won't go into the many ways people can manipulate and try to create guilt when you go after life in a way that makes you happy, but remember that these tactics are neither coming from intelligence nor love. You have as much a right as anyone to move forward with joy and create the life your soul guides you to.

You don't ever have to apologize about being true to yourself. Moving forward while following your joy is the path to happiness. When you act on the things inside that bring you joy, it raises your vibration to such a point that you become the best version of yourself. You'll also be able to offer the most value, because joy brings authenticity.

Think about it: do you like being around a person who is happy or miserable? I hope you answered happy, or it may be time to rethink who you're spending time with! Remember that energy is contagious! If this is a new way of thinking, don't beat yourself up. As human beings, we're messy sometimes and we don't even know why. *The great thing is that we can change at any time by changing our focus and moving forward from wherever we are.*

Practice joy every day. Have courage. You can do this.

5. Let go of what's out of your control.

As you move toward the best version of you, remember that while it's important to plan and take action, you also must learn to let go. You will face obstacles and challenges. Things will not always go your way. Some things won't work exactly as you thought. You may need to change your strategies from time to time. Some strategies will demonstrate that you have more work to do on yourself before you're ready for that step. Decide to keep moving forward *anyway*. Do what needs to be done. Sometimes the most challenging part of this is having patience *with yourself to not give up, no matter what.* Decide to let go of the need to control what you can't and focus instead on what you can control.

What you can control is you. Make your life your top priority. Care about becoming the best version of yourself until it consumes you. The better you are at being the best you, the more you can show up fully in your life, use your gifts, give to others, add value, and feel truly satisfied in your heart. Realizing what you can and can't control creates a sense of contrast. Contrast is always good because it gives you an opportunity to make a decision about what you will give your attention to: focusing on what you can control (you), or on what you can't (outside you).

Sometimes it's so easy to mind other people's business that we forget to mind our own. Remember, your greatest resources are your time and energy. Whatever you choose to focus on is an investment. If you're paying more attention to other people's lives than to your own, your focus will be scattered. Just as you can't chase two carrots at once, you won't get to where you want to go if you're not paying attention to your own path.

Taking back control of your life is just as much about knowing what we can't control as knowing what we can. Sometimes we're not even aware of how much time we spend trying to control things.

When my daughter was in kindergarten, we had a television in the kitchen where I would watch the morning news. At the time I didn't notice how distracted breakfast was because we'd be hearing stories of all sorts of tragic and awful things on the news. I often found myself switching the channel to spare my five-year-old's ears from countless disturbing stories. Over time, I realized how this not only took my focus away from my daughter but also brought negativity into the first thoughts of our day. I realized that while I couldn't control what went on in the news, I had *absolute* control over my own morning attention. So I gave up watching the news in the morning. Shortly after, I noticed how mornings felt more peaceful. Not allowing the energy of the news into my life was one of the best decisions I made. Today, morning meditations, visualizations, affirmations, writing, reading, and preparing for my day consume my attention, and I'm a more intentional person for it.

Every choice you make about what you give your attention to cultivates the garden where your thoughts will grow. Negativity will make your thoughts more negative. Positivity will cultivate a completely different vibration, and your thoughts and feelings will follow. Look at your focus and decide to focus on positive things. Everything you pay attention to feeds you in some way. Choose wisely.

WRAP UP

The thing about moving forward is that's all there really is. We move forward regardless whether we want to or not. The real choice is in ***how*** we move forward. Still, many of us think that by not taking steps forward we can somehow avoid pain or increase pleasure. The truth is that when you can embrace your todays and tomorrows with enthusiasm, you immediately shift the energy *that is your life*. Allow, flow, let go, and breathe.

When you realize that everything happening in your life is working *for* you, you can begin to feel safe to move forward. This moving forward motion *is* life itself. Getting intentional about making step-by-step progress toward your best self activates a magnetic energy that pulls other things toward you to help. All the things that show up in this synchronistic way become wonderful surprises that let you to know the Universe understands the language of being true to yourself. You need only be aware of the many ways you've always been supported. We all have so much to be thankful for, if we just notice. This is something to remind yourself of often.

LESSON 3 ASSIGNMENT

Below write down twenty feelings that you'd experience daily if you were moving forward and living as the best version of yourself.

1. _____

2. _____

3. _____

4. _____

5. _____

6. _____

7. _____

8. _____

9. _____

10. _____

11. _____

12. _____

13. _____

14. _____

15. _____

16. _____

17. _____

18. _____

19. _____

20. _____

Extra Credit:

To experience these feelings every day, write them down somewhere else (index cards are good) and read them three times a day. Spend a few minutes every day thinking of how you can cultivate these feelings and experience more of them. Learn to line up with what feels good and move forward in that direction.

THE LESSON OF PERSISTENCE

Patience, persistence and perspiration make an unbeatable combination for success.

—Napolean Hill

When you set out to accomplish something, you will come up against situations that put your persistence to the test. Things can be going along fine and then out of nowhere, something happens and turns your world on its head. It's usually not planned, and definitely not welcomed…life gets messy. During these times, we respond by either giving up or growing and getting up.

At an especially busy time in my life and business, my landlord texted me that the place I'd been renting for the previous four years would be going on the market in two weeks. My heart sank. I cried and didn't sleep that night. I ran my home, business, and office out of where I lived. Being a realtor, I knew all too well the inconveniences of needing to leave the house often to show properties. Also, I had absolutely NO IDEA if the buyers would want me to move out. A little text sent me into a fearful tizzy because my world was being shaken up and I had no control. My thoughts were controlling me and not in a positive way. The next day, I prayed and asked for guidance, favor, and wisdom. What power I *did* have was in how I chose to handle myself. Despite my initial meltdown, I knew that I wanted to be strong and have faith. Recalling all of the things that had worked out in my life even when I was fearful, I reminded myself that I would be OK no matter what. Knowing the weeks ahead would be busy, I also decided to increase my self-care. I made sure to get enough sleep by going to bed earlier, I ate really healthy, clean foods, went back into therapy, scheduled time with positive friends who always made me feel good, walked my dog, took time to read, and even scheduled in a massage. I realized I had to be there for me!

To close the loop, all of the worst things I'd imagined never happened. My new landlord was happy for me to stay, didn't increase my rent, and ended up making many improvements to the property.

It's wonderful to get the support from others, but I've also found that sometimes you have to give it to yourself! Persistence in being the best version of yourself counts even more during times when you want to unravel.

Merriam-Webster's dictionary defines persistence as "the action or fact of persisting."

This is a big one. Persistence is essential if you intend to be fulfilled and experience your desired outcome. Be prepared to take on a few flesh wounds along the way. Life happens, and sometimes it can seem to derail your efforts to focus and move forward. Don't be surprised!

Your persistence is intimately connected to your outcome.

This isn't a fair-weathered connection either. This connection between your persistence and your outcome must be like a near obsession to persevere until completion. It's about improving your life through creation. Creation is intense. Nature shows us just how raw, fierce, and relentless creation really is. Keep this in mind as you set on your way to change something in your life.

FIVE QUESTIONS TO IDENTIFY A LACK OF PERSISTENCE

1. Do you frequently procrastinate? Putting things off till tomorrow, but often never getting things done?

2. When obstacles or challenges present themselves, do you complain and cast blame?

3. When you see other people being successful, do you think it came easy for them, or that they have a secret shortcut?

4. Do you fail to create plans and put them into action because of what other people would think, do, or say?

5. Do you let past mistake define what you're capable of now?

If you were honest and said yes to some of these questions, guess what? You're not alone! We've all found ways (often unknowingly) to avoid persisting toward a more satisfying life. This isn't about beating yourself up, but about learning how to become better! Life is a never-ending project, and although you will never *arrive*, the goal is to enjoy your journey while working on becoming the best version of yourself you possibly can! Being persistent will show you just how much you're capable of!

FIVE METHODS TO CULTIVATE PERSISTENCE

Building muscles of persistence is how you improve your life. Every day, remind yourself of what achieving your ideal outcome will do for your life and how it will make you feel. You'll need to call upon this driving emotion when some days turn into a *shift* show.

1. Do It Now

Windows of opportunity do two things: they open, and they close. Your time and energy are actually *opportunities* that you're able to use and invest in any way you'd like. One of the major differences between successful and unsuccessful people is how they embrace and focus on their opportunities. You have 1,440 minutes in a day, just like everybody else. How you use these minutes will determine the quality of your life.

Procrastination is a dream killer. For years I was a master procrastinator. Honestly, I thought it wasn't a big deal, and things always could wait. As I got older I realized that the areas I hadn't improved were a source of low self-esteem. I began to doubt myself and questioned if I'd ever improve. What followed were years of authentically working on healing myself and loving myself enough to know my life was worth it. I realized I was the one responsible for my attitudes and choices, even the ones that never served me.

Becoming willing to change was actually a beautiful point of surrender. Even when I made mistakes, I remained persistent in the reconditioning of my mind. After years of procrastinating, it was uncomfortable at first, but it became easier as I began to take steps forward. Experiencing something painful can be an opportunity to decide to change for the better.

Try one small act a day of learning something new, acquiring a new skill, reading a book to enhance your knowledge, spending time with someone who can teach you something…done consistently, this adds up to 365 successful acts a year! Now do two things a day and that's 730 successful acts a year…or five a day for 1,825 successful acts a year! Talk about compound interest!

How good would you feel if your goal was to get a healthy body, and every day for a year you'd do one, two, three, four, or five successful things? Things like working out, eliminating processed foods, trying a new healthy recipe, listening to a podcast on habits of healthy people, going for a walk, getting off sugar, or envisioning yourself as the healthiest you've ever been! You'd be a different person. This is how changing your life works. You've got to persist on good days, bad days, rainy days, snowy days, tired days, and every day. *You can do this!!*

If you made a list of the things that matter to you most, trust me when I say that procrastination won't be on it. It's best to kick the habit to the curb now, while you are becoming aware that it does nothing but hold you back. It's OK that you are where you are; it's just not OK that you stay where you are. It's time to get off the sidelines and jump into the game of your life!

2. Take 100 Percent Responsibility

Taking 100 percent responsibility gives you leverage because it means acknowledging that you have a choice. When we blame and complain, there might be some momentary gratification, but at the end of the day it's only going to keep you stuck and powerless. It's only a habit, and you can break any habit by starting a new one.

Taking 100 percent responsibility means owning whatever experience you're having right now. You might not believe this, but our invisible murmurings and complaints are indeed heard by the Universe, which delivers the kind of energy we've directed out *back to us*. This also includes complaining about yourself! Being the best you is nearly impossible when you are so focused on what's wrong. Persistence requires focusing on loving and supporting your best self. This is a very different energy than blaming and complaining.

This reminds me of a time in my early twenties when I really unhappy. I hated my job, and it was a very turbulent time in my life. This jagged energy matched my job. Every day felt like drudgery. I felt like I was walking into a prison. Of course, it wasn't a prison, but mentally I felt shut down. I remember blaming and complaining to my friends about how awful the women at my work were and how terrible I felt.

Knowing that my life was in disarray, I decided I needed to make a change toward something that felt like living again. Going out for lunch one day, I drove away and just kept driving. Something that felt like freedom in my spirit happened, and I never went back. Although I tell this story to illustrate how what was happening on the outside was a reflection of my internal state, I'm not recommending this as a good way to leave a place of employment. However, there is a point where enough is enough. The place pulled me into a place of negativity, and although I'd attracted it, I also made a choice to leave it. Being jobless wasn't the best choice either, but when I look back all I remember is the feeling of doing something. I was willing to turn and walk away, even though there were certainly better ways I could have gone about it.

This experience helped me realize that we have to be persistent in our thinking to move forward to something better, no matter what poor decisions we have made in the past. Today my persistence is in making decisions that line up with whatever moves me toward the best version of myself. This isn't always easy. Sometimes it's hard to explain why we must end a chapter or move on. It's just something we *feel* inside.

The biggest gift of taking 100 percent responsibility for our lives and everything we experience is that we can be confident and trust ourselves again. Knowing we can change anything is powerful. When we commit to persistence, our inner warrior wakes up. You don't have to be a victim unless you choose to. This means letting go of the blame-and-complain game. Forever.

Everything going on in your life is meant to show you where you're on and where you're off track. In the story I shared earlier, I was very off. I had attracted all sorts of experiences that mirrored my own negativity and victim-thinking. At the time, I didn't realize I was manifesting it and therefore it continued...until I looked inside to address the real issues. It's actually a relief to come to this place. It felt like a surrender I was ready for. You can look all over the world for solutions to your problems, but until you look within it always feels just a little out of reach.

3. You're Going to Have to Work for It

Think of athletes or people with high levels of training in nearly every field. There is an intense focus and an unwavering will to dedicate each and every day to their desired outcome. There are no short cuts. Their every cell knows the dedication, sacrifice, and pain this requires. They can't play small. They accept that they're going to have to work for it. Every day, no excuses.

When opportunity comes, you need to be prepared. Every day, you have a chance to prepare. Persistence is essential. Every day presents another invitation.

Persistence pairs well with visualization. When you take five to fifteen minutes each day to visualize the actual outcome, it's super powerful. Over time, this becomes so familiar to you that it just seems natural. This practice is worth cultivating. Whatever you focus on, especially emotionally, it is like cleaning foggy glasses to see with perfect clarity. The clearer you are, the more directed your focus, and the more certain your outcome!

Part of knowing you have to work for whatever you want in your life means counting the cost and becoming proactive in managing issues *before* they become a problem. When you expect adjustments, then you make whatever decisions you need to *beforehand* so you don't run into crisis! This is an empowering way of handling any challenges that may present themselves.

I remember one summer, I was crazy busy. Besides running three businesses, I was adjusting to the new summer schedule after my daughter got out of school. I was also focusing on a couple workshops I'd be giving within the next month, as well as writing. I valued any extra time, but I didn't want to miss out on spending one-on-one time with my daughter either. After some thought, we had a conversation where I shared with her what I was doing to reach my goal of getting this book published, while also emphasizing that I valued our time together. My plan was go with the flow as much as we could during the week, but on Sundays we'd head out on a day-trip adventure together. She agreed. It solved my concern while adding value into not only our lives as individuals, but also into our mother/daughter relationship.

Situations like this are what make me absolutely sure that our level of persistence is what *makes us care enough to prepare* for your ideal outcome, including the challenges along the way. This is living with intentional awareness, meaning that you're making your life what you want it to be, *while* exercising personal development skills through your awareness of what is happening as a result. *Do not think it is a little thing to master the art of yourself.*

Life is an exceptional classroom filled with lessons on how to adapt to change, make decisions, shift gears, balance your time, and so much more. So many of the things that fill up our days never bring us any closer to our ideal outcome or true fulfillment. Your job is to find what works and what doesn't to make your life fulfilling. By the way, this doesn't end at retirement. This is a way of life that sets you apart from the apathy that has affected far too many adults, who never dream of their ideal outcomes.

Creating a visual picture of persistence is one last concept I'd like to share with you in this section. I'm going to take you to a place where you can imagine the kind of persistence you'll need to follow through to the end of your goal outcome. That place is in *Game of Thrones* (hopefully you've seen it!), the very popular show on HBO.

Remember Drogo and Daenerys? I want you to picture your ideal outcome as Drogo. This ideal outcome is huge and fierce and will not take any of your crap. It could kill you, but you can't look away. The intensity is beast-like even when calm. You know this dream is going to create a life shift, but you say eff to fear and comfort and make the decision to say yes to persistence and go for it anyway! This decision is you saying yes to the habit of persistence toward your ideal outcome.

Now I want you to think of Daenerys as your decision (persistence). Beautiful and somewhat unsure of what her union to Drogo will mean, she has an inner strength that does not waver. In the beginning of their marriage, Drogo (your ideal outcome) was a beast with Daenerys (your decision to say yes to the habit of persistence toward your ideal outcome). He was on top, and she couldn't do much.

It can feel just like this in the beginning of settling into the daily practice of keeping your intention clear, while moving forward with many small steps. If anyone tells you it's all peaches and roses, they're lying. But it's good because you'll need to learn new things and break complex things down in a way you've never done before. You'll need both your ideal outcome *and* your persistence.

Daenerys, out of her persistence and desiring a particular outcome, asked and learned how to be a skilled lover. You want to charm your Drogo (your ideal outcome) like that too. When you are intimate with someone you love, you are focused, present, and feeling a lot of amazing emotions (hopefully)! Her focus and decision to be the best damn lover in the world was powerful to say the least! This turned her from dominated to dominator, a fierce lover in the truest sense. Daenerys wouldn't accept things as they were, and she got better, which made the whole relationship better. Now it's true that Drogo dies in the show, but you can imagine the energy those two stirred up and use it to lean into your practicing the habit of persistence.

Living this habit of persistence towards your ideal outcome will give your life whole new meaning. You got this!

4. Have Faith

Having faith means having complete trust and confidence in yourself, while believing there is more around the corner than what you can see right now. It's also knowing that you have unseen resources in your favor. Faith must be activated from inside.

One of my favorite books, *A Course in Miracles*, has a lesson that I often find myself reading when my faith wavers. In the *Workbook for Students*, Lesson 47 says, "God is the strength in which I trust." This statement tells me that my faith wavers when I rely solely on my own strength. You can tell you're relying on your own strength when you experience fear. Whether you use the term God, Source, Universe, Life Force, or whatever, it all points to the place we originated from before we took on this physical form. I believe this bigger place is always connected to us and available to us if we are willing to accept it.

Knowing there is a strength far greater than mine that I can trust completely changes my view of any obstacle. All of us have experienced times when our backs are up against a wall and we literally need a miracle. This is the exact time to ask your Source for help. Help can come in the form of an idea, guidance, a friend calling with some helpful information, an intuition, or practically anything that comes as a response. When you turn away from your limited view and have faith in a power greater than yourself, you can expect the most amazing miracles.

Ignoring this connection to the Source, which is available to all of us, is one reason we get so overwhelmed at times. When I forget to turn to the Source is when I become paralyzed by fear. It is also a strong determining factor in how things are going to work out...or not. It isn't always comfortable to trust something you can't see, but this is exactly what having faith means.

Believing in something that's possible even though it hasn't been part of your experience so far is how faith keeps you going. When you have it, you can sense there's an X-factor involved. It isn't all on your shoulders. There's a bigger plan for your life that you can't see but that you can *feel*. Learning to have faith in yourself is not something many people were taught growing up, often because there was a bigger belief in fear. Having faith doesn't mean you never feel fear, but it means you trust that whatever is in your heart to do/be/have was put there for you to tend and grow.

It can be challenging when people close to us don't believe we can do something. Some people may think, do, or say things that are unkind, and then you let your feelings get hurt because you've looked more to these outside opinions than to your own heart. Caring too much about what other people think will make you second guess yourself. Basing your true potential on others' limited points of view is crazy. You must learn to care more about how *you feel* than what anyone else thinks of you. Other people's opinions of you are none of your business anyway.

We all set the bar for what we expect. When the bar is raised, it's amazing what we can do. When your bar is set low, people around you may want to stay comfortable and become uncomfortable if you raise your bar and leave them where they are. That's why it's so important to surround yourself with people who believe in you. People can influence you in a positive way and help you move toward your best self. Or they can negatively influence you to doubt yourself, feel down, and even give up on your dreams.

According to the Bible, "Faith is the substance of things hoped for, the evidence of things not seen." (Hebrews 11:1)

If you're truly to have faith, you're going to need persistence. We all have setbacks, but after the initial shock, you must look up and move forward. Everyone has greatness within them. Everyone has ideas waiting to be nurtured into inventions, better relationships, books, business models, solutions to problems, art, love, and making the world a better place.

Sometimes we don't see the great potential within ourselves because we judge ourselves on how we've identified ourselves in the past. You get no credit for dragging your past with you. It's unfair when the present moment doesn't have its own chance to shine, without yesterday raining on its parade. Sometimes you just have to let things go. Believe in yourself and have faith that you're unique and your gifts are valuable. Work to bring out the best in yourself each and every day. Your faith will be rewarded.

5. Do Just One Thing Every Day

When we move toward improving an area of our lives, it's easy to get overwhelmed and feel like you don't have enough time and energy. You might look back and see times where you've tried something and it didn't work. Remembering how you felt can stop you before you even get started. But remember: right now is completely new. Right here, right now is whatever *you* decide it to be. To get back on track to making progress simplify, simplify, simplify.

If you make it a habit to do just one thing every day, over time, it will add up. You don't need to expect major life changes to happen quickly. In fact, I've often found the opposite is true. Writing this book has taken longer than I'd ever thought, and sometimes it felt like it was taking forever. Despite the delays, as long as I made one step toward its progress every day, I felt satisfaction in the forward movement itself. Sometimes we want to arrive somewhere before we've taken the proper steps to earn it. Something isn't a failure because it takes longer than we first thought. It takes time, patience, energy, mindset, and persistence to bring something to life.

Learning a new language, becoming a better partner, learning how to invest financially, creating a new income opportunity, training for a triathlon, putting yourself out there to follow your dreams...all these things take time. Sometimes even when you might feel ready, other elements may not be. It's an ebb and flow; a give and take. Some days you will make significant progress, and other days you'll feel frustrated for not doing as much as you set out to. No matter what happens, every day just decide to do one thing. And do this one thing as well as you possibly can. If you're trying to get healthier, make that healthy meal with love. When you eat it, fill your heart with gratitude and enjoy every bite. Make your efforts special by realizing that for every one thing you do, you're that much closer to the person you want to be.

Right where you are is the perfect place to begin. There is no better time than now. There is no one to better live the best version of yourself than you. Believe that doing just one thing toward your goals every day will build momentum inside of you. This momentum will build confidence. Over time, being consistent and persistent will become strong muscles.

WRAP UP

Persistence is a mindset that, once embraced, fuels you with endurance for the achievement of anything you set out to accomplish. Living to just barely get by won't get you to your dreams. Before you embark on any journey, you must count the cost. Any dream will cost you in terms of your time and energy. Making a decision up front to be persistent will help you on days when things don't seem to be going your way. Life happens, and sometimes it is messier than we'd like. Wherever your destination may be, decide to start now. Take 100 percent responsibility. Know that you're going to have to work for it. Have faith. And every day, just make sure to do one thing well toward your goal.

LESSON 4 ASSIGNMENT

1. If you commit to non-negotiable persistence, describe five things you'd be doing differently toward achieving your goals.

    1. _____
    _____

    2. _____
    _____

    3. _____
    _____

    4. _____
    _____

    5. _____
    _____

THE LESSON OF NEUTRALIZING

The acquirement and enjoyment of physical well-being, mental calm and spiritual peace are priceless to their possessors...

—Joseph Pilates

To learn to neutralize areas of your life is, in essence, to apply balance to what could potentially hold you back from living the best you. Let's take food as an example. When people talk about alkalinity, they're referring to the pH balance in the body. Scientifically, pH is the balance of the positively charged hydrogen ion molecules in our body and refers to the acid and base balance in our blood, saliva, or mucus. This relationship between acid and base (or pH) is measured on a scale from 1 to 14, with 7 being neutral, below 7 being acidic, and above 7 being alkaline.

In a nutshell, our bodies benefit by maintaining a neutral or slightly alkaline state for optimal health. An acidic body can make us vulnerable to disease. High acidity has been linked to fatigue, depression, poor digestion, candida, weight retention, headaches, and muscle/joint pain.

Neutralizing a potentially very acidic body is beneficial because you need health to live as the best version of you! Today's society has become predominately acidic. Acidification of your body causes inflammation,

Sheryl Corriveau

which is the beginning of nearly every unwanted physical condition. This acidic state is largely because we are disconnected to what we put into our bodies and minds. It's not mainstream in our culture to understand this vital connection, but it can be changed. The first thing to do is *make the decision that you must feel good!* **Think of neutralizing as offsetting anything acidic in your life, in order to feel better.**

Feeling good and having the energy to live your life well means that you have to take care of your body and mind. Eating lots of greens will help to neutralize acid in your body. If you stay away from sugar, you'll save yourself tons of trouble from problems like being overweight, having joint pain, inflammation, skin issues, digestive issues, depression, and more acidic conditions. I know the thought of eliminating sugar sounds completely nuts. But most people who do it quickly realize how amazing they feel and how much more energy they have.

After my daughter was born, I wanted to lose the baby weight. At the time, someone who I've always loved, the late Wayne Dyer, had shared how he'd lost over twenty pounds himself by reducing his sugar intake to less than thirty grams a day. Feeling inspired, I cut sugar almost completely out of my life. For a whole year and a half, I kept my sugar consumption under twenty-five grams a day (this could easily be one serving size of certain fruits!). After two weeks, I no longer craved sugar AT ALL. Not only was I able to quickly lose all the baby weight, but I looked and felt better than I had in years! After researching sugar's effects, I was amazed on the havoc it truly wreaks in our lives. Today I'm a lot less extreme, but I still try to make consuming sugar the exception rather than the rule.

The definition of neutralizing in this context means to render (something) ineffective or harmless by applying an opposite force or effect.

The practice of neutralizing applies not only to the types of food you eat, but especially to the thoughts we have.

There's tremendous energy in our words. The energy behind the words we say, and the thoughts behind them, are either helping us or hurting us. It's an invisible energy, so it's easy to forget that it's there. But it's everywhere, in everything, and everyone...even in the air itself. When you tune into the truth behind the effects of some of the thoughts we think, you can literally feel which are beneficial or harmful. The effects of our thoughts and words can profoundly affect our experience in life. In fact, they impact every area of what you believe is true about yourself.

Please pay attention to the words that come out of your mouth and really ask yourself: *Is the energy in the words I'm saying moving me toward a more fulfilling life?*

An even better question is: *Is the energy I'm experiencing bringing me closer or further from me being able to show up as the best me?*

You can't constantly focus on what is causing you a lack of fulfillment and expect how you feel to change. So many times, we continue telling ourselves a story we don't like about something in our lives, but the idea never occurs to us to change the story. It may be an area you don't realize you can change, but you can! In this chapter, I'll share some ways to begin neutralizing your life from the inside out!

FIVE QUESTIONS TO IDENTIFY A NEED FOR NEUTRALIZING

1. Do you often consume processed foods with a shelf life longer than yours?

2. Do you often feel tired and lethargic?

3. Do you feel overwhelmed and cluttered in your environment?

4. Do the people you surround yourself with make you feel powerful or powerless?

5. Do the conversations you have with yourself reflect the best or worst version of yourself?

If answering some of these questions brought up some things about your life that you'd like to change, you're in the exact place you need to be to start going where you want to go! Change begins with seeing parts of our lives that we'd like to improve and then moving forward in the direction that will give us a different experience. Neutralizing your life will improve it with measureable results!

FIVE METHODS TO CREATING MORE NEUTRALIZING

1. Eat for ROI

In order to neutralize your body, start with the foods you eat. My basic goal is to receive a return on investment, or ROI, for the foods I consume. If you regularly eat food devoid of minerals and nutrients, you could be full but your cells are starving. For this reason, I like to think of food in terms of the life energy it will give back to me. There's a book I read called *Superfoods* by David Wolfe. In it, he discusses Kirlian photography, which basically shows the living energy of an object. In this case, the pictures are of food.

Kirlian photography is a method of photographically capturing the aura of energy that emanates from animals and plants and that undergoes changes in accordance with physiological or emotional changes. Seeing food in terms of the kind of life energy it contains sheds a very different light on the kind of ROI we get from consuming it.

Everyone's bodies are different, and I personally don't subscribe to a one-size-fits-all view when it comes to nutrition. What I do believe is that to be healthy, you must learn to listen to your body and develop an understanding of what foods it needs and when it needs them. By really listening to your body, especially how you feel after you eat a certain food, you will discover what is best for you.

Generally speaking, minerals and nutrients are essential for your cells to be the best they can be. Eating as close to how Nature created food will give you a much better ROI than fast food or processed stuff that basically leaves you undernourished.

Scientific research and personal experience both prove that what we eat affects how we think and how we act. One of the easiest ways to improve your ROI is to read food labels and don't eat anything you can't pronounce. Stick to whole foods that will feed your body the way Nature intended.

Every time you eat you can simply slow down and think about what kind of energy you will benefit from most. When you want to feel lighter, go for greens and foods that energetically feel light. When you want to feel more grounded, maybe go more for root vegetables that energetically feel more grounded. Over time, you'll begin to enjoy your relationship with food as an empowering way to lean toward what would make you feel best.

An excellent book to give you a broader comprehension of the energy of food through illustrated charts is *The Truth About Food; The Good, The Bad and The Downright Dangerous* by Gillian Drake.

2. Neutralize Your Energy

One simple way to neutralize low energy is by oxygenating your body through movement. Often feeling tired can almost seem normal because life can get so busy. Although it may initially feel counterintuitive, getting a daily workout will, in fact, give you *more* energy. The most common excuse I hear is, "I don't have the time." The truth is, we all have the same amount of time every day, but it's up to you how you invest it. Fifteen minutes a day can make a huge difference in your life.

Personally, I've been practicing Pilates on the Reformer for years, as well as teaching Pilates and PiYO classes, hiking trails, and often doing some streaming video workouts from YouTube or Beachbody when I need some cardio to get my sweat on. It really is just about moving your body and getting more oxygen in! When you get more oxygen, you feel better, have more energy, and relieve stress. If you don't have a regular movement time in your day, it's the perfect time to start! Take classes, find a friend to walk or run with, sign up with a personal trainer, or check out the plethora of YouTube videos with just about every form of exercise you can imagine!

There's one form of movement I often recommend, and it's called rebounding. If you're not familiar with the rebounder, it's a mini trampoline. NASA did a study and showed that the rebounder is 68 percent more effective as a cardiovascular exercise for weight loss than running (NASA, *Journal of Applied Physiology* 49 (5): 881-887).

Some benefits of the rebounder:

- Boosts your immune system by circulating lymphatic fluid
- Strengthens cells due to an increase in oxygen flow to cells
- Improves heart and lung function similar to or better than other aerobic activities
- Is easy on the knees and other joints because of the shock absorption of the trampoline
- Detoxifies via lymphatic drainage

Personally, I don't have a specific routine when using my rebounder. It's very simple: just get on and start jumping, varying your arm and leg movements. I keep one in my office so that when I need a quick break, I can hop on for even five minutes and I feel so much better! If you're concerned about balance, there are even types of rebounders that have a bar to hold onto if you need it. The important thing is to make it a daily habit by setting a time each day to do it. Fifteen minutes may not seem like much, but in one week that's over an hour and a half. Neutralize any low energy by getting your *move* on!

3. Clean Up Clutter

I believe everything is energy. How you feel is affected by everything in your life, especially your environment. I've noticed that when I'd let my office get cluttered and unorganized, I feel cluttered and unorganized. It's not an official term, but I'd say it was an *acidic environment,* because it didn't feel good. One of the decisions I made was that in order to be and think at my best, clutter must go. I'm not saying this is easy, because we tend to collect too much stuff. Over time, the stuff begins to grow until its energy feels rather burdensome. This is an area that will yield immediate benefits of neutralizing!

There's a great book I highly recommend called, *The Life Changing Habit of Tidying Up: The Japanese Art of Decluttering and Organizing* by Marie Kondo. It basically says for each item in your life, ask if you truly love it and use it. If not, it goes.

Being attached to "stuff" can prevent better things, opportunities, and ideas from entering your life. Neutralizing is all about feeling good. Acidic energy, over time, affects your confidence and what's possible for your life. Psychologically, when you can't get a handle on your clutter, your belief will be "I can't do it." Over time, this will spill over into other areas of your life. Self-doubt grows the same way self-confidence does...by your daily choices.

University of New Mexico's Catherine Roster and colleagues (2016) examined how clutter compromises an individual's perception of home and ultimately feelings of satisfaction with life. Roster defined "home" not simply as the physical dwelling in which you live, but more generally as "the broader constellation of experiences, meanings, and situations that shape and are actively shaped by a person in the creation of his or her lifeworld."

It doesn't matter how long clutter may have been lingering around—set a day or weekend on your calendar to start decluttering. Complete decluttering one area of your space at a time. No matter how long it takes, it will be so well worth it! In terms of clutter, less is definitely more!

If you find you have emotional attachments to your clutter, you may even want to hire a professional organizer to come in and help you. If you have someone who lives with you and has a lot of clutter, you will have to address this. Working with someone else to deal with their clutter can be even more difficult than dealing with your own issues. However, it may have to be done to get your home clutter-free and get you on your path to peace.

Cleaning up your clutter is no different than raising your standards anywhere in life. Any great ideas and intentions for bettering yourself have a lifespan of their own. You must capture them as they come and *take immediate action*. Unless a life crisis or a major event happens in your life that wakes you up, you'll go through life stuck in stories you no longer want. Whatever reason you have for keeping clutter in your life is just another acidic story. It may seem harsh if you're not used to learning how to rein in these cumbersome stories, but it is necessary if you want to live a fulfilling life.

4. Neutralize Your Associations

You've heard it before that if you want to know where you're going, look at who you surround yourself. Motivational speaker Jim Rohn famously said that we are the average of the five people we spend the most time with. Who we surround ourselves with affects our self-esteem, decision-making, and influences how we see life. By association, you can grow toward the best version of yourself, or you can be held back.

There are times when you will realize you will only go so far spending time with certain people. It's not that anyone is a bad person, or that anyone is better than anyone else; but some people's energy *will* hinder your progress. This is simply because they have settled at whatever level they're at, and self-improvement isn't their goal. Run, don't walk away from these people.

Energy is contagious, and we all share our energy with others, whether it's knowingly or not. After spending time with someone, check in with yourself and ask how you feel after engaging with that person's energy. Notice how this energy affects your mood, mind, and thoughts.

It's important to realize how meaningful it is to spend time with people who are also on their own path to becoming the best version of themselves. Their energy will inspire and uplift you, pulling you even more quickly toward becoming a better version of yourself.

I can recall distinct times that I'd experienced uncomfortable feelings, ending relationships that I'd allowed to take root in my life. As the years went on, and I continued to work on myself, I could see how I began to attract people on a similar life path of self-improvement. Once you know what you want out of your life, you will want to surround yourselves with others who share your core values.

Leveling up and raising your standards continuously, in order to stretch your limits and lean into your edge, requires a certain type of mindset that isn't the norm. Many people do not care about improving their lives. So many excuses roll off as to why they *can't*. You don't want to be around the "*I can't*" types of attitudes. If you don't feel you have the types of people who inspire you to be your best self, start becoming the *person* you want to attract. Over time, the energy you put out will attract the right people to you.

Remember that every relationship is a teaching/learning opportunity. By being around those you admire and respect, you will begin to adopt positive characteristics. Likewise, if you've experienced others who have demonstrated a personality trait that left a distasteful energy, you can learn by example what it is you'd like to avoid in your own character. Make every experience something you can learn from, and make sure that no opportunity is ever wasted.

Remember that everyone, including you, is doing the best they can for where they're at emotionally, spiritually, mentally, physically, and in their current state of awareness and perception. We can forgive ourselves and others as we build the foundations for new, improved chapters in our lives.

Relationships help us grow, and each one can be an opportunity to say thank you. When neutralizing this area, remember that even in letting go, you can be thankful for the experience.

5. Choose Your Words Wisely

Let's *feel* these words. Sense whether these words need some neutralizing:

Hate

Love

Disgusting

Beautiful

Stupid

Intelligent

Fear

Faith

Powerless

Powerful

The reason you need to realize how powerful and emotional the words you say are is because they shape and design your world. The words you say are directly related to whether you reach your greatest potential or not. They have a vibration of their own and will attract the same kind of energy. Whether consciously or not, you're constantly absorbing and sharing energy from the thoughts you think.

Always ask yourself: ***Are these thoughts moving me toward or away from my ideal outcome?*** What feels good is always neutralizing. What feels bad is acidic. Begin to pay attention to how things *feel*. You want to align with as many neutralizing emotions as you can. This most definitely is affected by the words spoken by you and to you. For this very reason, I avoid watching the news or anything violent that takes me away from how I intentionally choose to feel.

Don't be surprised if some ego resistance pops up with this. You are reining in a thought system that has never been managed and used effectively. It's important to know that you give life to your thoughts by making them a reality.

Thoughts on their own are meaningless until you give them a meaning. The good news is *you can* change your thoughts. If something you're thinking feels bad, sad, overwhelming, discouraging, etc., decide to look elsewhere. Change the channel. Get out of where you're sitting and look around to see the good. There is always something good. It's up to you to focus on it.

Do not settle for an untrained thought system. Choose thoughts that feel better.

Emotion is "energy in motion." When someone experiences negative emotions, there is a physical drainage of energy. That's how your thoughts become catalysts that can make you sick and tired. When you start producing negativity with your thoughts, this will activate the law of attraction to bring you more of the same. If these thoughts are not neutralized and eliminated, they can create serious health challenges. Positive emotions, such as love, peace, hope, faith, and forgiveness, can all be neutralizing to your body's entire energetic system. The negative emotions of anger, resentment, and fear are the most powerful of all draining emotions. The fear of the unknown is probably the most powerful and depleting of them all.

Since your thoughts govern your emotions, you want to surround yourself with as many positive experiences that can be taken in by all five senses.

Every day I diffuse essential oils that create pleasant smells and offer changing, soft lights that are easy on my eyes. I also make time to meditate, journal, exercise, read, spend time in nature, and stay connected to people who I love and bring me joy. All of my five senses (and actually my sixth, intuition) feel good with these daily rituals. It doesn't happen by chance. It happens by choice.

Choose your thoughts constantly, and only entertain the thoughts that serve you best. Don't believe in excuses that mask themselves as stories as to why you need to stay in a negative or stuck place. Get on with it, darlin'!

Good thoughts attract more good-feeling experiences, while negative thoughts are repelling and constricting, attracting more negative experiences. Happy people have made the choice to be happy. It doesn't mean they don't experience challenges like anyone else, but they *choose what they focus on and how they interpret what happens to them*. It's all a matter of perception.

We can choose our own perception by choosing to cultivate these positive feelings daily:

Love and Warmth

Appreciation and Gratitude

Childlike Curiosity

Excitement and Passion

Determination

Flexibility

Confidence / Faith

Cheerfulness

Feeling Healthy

Sense of contribution

The only way to accomplish this is through consistent effort and conscious choosing. You will feel what you focus on.

WRAP UP

When embarking on creating the habit to create more neutralizing in your physical body and thoughts, you will naturally push up against the

ACID. What I mean is that this endeavor to change your level of fulfill-ment, happiness, joy, peace, or anything else that is currently occupied by *not that* (aka: ACID) will bump up against some parts of yourself that will be resistant. Anything that's been given permission to take root in your mind and life will fight to stay. The fight is called discomfort. This is the exact place where many people give up. To be aware of this process is to understand that it's natural to feel this way.

Patience is the key. Simply allow yourself to be patient with yourself. No matter what ideal outcomes you've set, it's going to take however long it takes. Choosing to adopt patience *beforehand* will aid in the stretching that will happen inside you along your journey.

The other HUGE part of having a neutralizing experience is to embrace ENJOYING THE WHOLE RIDE. You choose to enjoy the bookkeeping, the bills to pay, the dishes to wash, the unexpected cancellation, AND the synchronicity that it gave to you to take a walk with a friend you would've missed! Enjoying your life is very stylish and very neutralizing! Find ways to enjoy every part of your day.

LESSON 5 ASSIGNMENT

1. List five things you can take action on immediately to create more neutralizing in your body and thoughts:

    1. _____
    2. _____
    3. _____
    4. _____
    5. _____

2. List five ways you can take action today to eliminate acidity in your body and thoughts:

    1. _____
    _____

2. _____

_____

3. _____

_____

4. _____

_____

5. _____

_____

THE LESSON OF LISTENING

> I remind myself every morning: Nothing I say this day will teach me
> anything. So if I'm going to learn, I must do it by listening.
>
> **—Larry King**

A while back, life was busy as usual, but I had felt for a while that I'd
been burning the candle at both ends. After a busy morning of working
with clients, I drove to pick up my daughter and then had a couple of show-
ings for real estate scheduled after that. After I picked her up, something
unexpected happened when I went to get back in my car. Suddenly I felt
faint and couldn't drive. Then out of nowhere, I started crying. There was
nothing really wrong, or so I thought initially. It lasted maybe a good five
minutes. After gathering myself, I left feeling shaken.

After this happened, I was pretty freaked out and worried that something might be wrong. That next week, I went to my doctor to have some
tests done and see what was going on. Truth be told, I'd felt so healthy
that I hadn't been to see my doctor in quite a while, and I wasn't even sure
of which door to go in at the "new" building they had moved into three
years before.

After several tests, my doctor concluded there was nothing wrong. I knew I needed to quiet down and listen to what my body was trying to tell me. I came to the conclusion that my experience was my body's way of slowing me down. What had happened was a physical reaction to my need to slow down and live in a more balanced way. I knew this was something I'd been feeling for quite some time, and now my body had my full attention. It was liberating, really, to have a legit "reason" to take better care of myself. And I don't mean on the outside, but on the inside. My body made me listen to what my intuition had been trying to tell me. Looking within, I knew that doing too much was why I couldn't listen to my intuition until I experienced a meltdown.

Sometimes trying to do too much actually leaves you behind. From this point on, I began to cut back on what I allowed in my scheduler. This allowed me to move ahead on my most important goals, including writing this book.

Scaling back in order to focus on my most important thing has taught me a valuable lesson. Scattering energy in all directions like shrapnel leaves you nearly powerless. In order to get ahead, you must learn to listen to your inner guidance. A great book that helped drive this point home and I highly recommend is *The One Thing* by Gary Keller.

Have you ever had something happen that forced you to listen because up until that point, life just seemed to pull you in many different directions, while you felt powerless to slow down or change it? This brings us to lesson five, the lesson of listening.

Merriam-Webster's dictionary defines listening as "to hear something with thoughtful attention: give consideration."

FIVE QUESTIONS TO IDENTIFY A LACK OF LISTENING

1. Do you freeze out what your intuition is saying?
2. Do you act as if you don't know what to do, when it's really that you're scared to do it?
3. Do you feel blocked and not able to hear your intuition?

4. Do you think the answers are always outside of you?

5. Are you always pleasing others instead of yourself?

If you've answered YES to any of these questions, you're among nearly 100 percent of our society. We have grown so accustomed to living at such an accelerated pace that many of us have almost completely drowned out the voice of our beautiful intuition. But there is a way to reconnect and realign with the truest part of ourselves. This part has so much wisdom and guidance to share with us!

FIVE METHODS TO LISTEN

1. Align with Your Intuition

I had never been taught to listen to my own internal guidance. In theory it sounded good, but in practical application it felt threatening because it went against my ego. Listening to my intuition telling me I desperately needed to slow down was followed by disappointment and sadness because it simply didn't seem possible. So I kept pushing, ignoring my inner guidance. Have you ever felt this way?

Then something inevitably happens. Maybe our health takes a dive when we've known we needed to eat better and exercise more, but we ignored it. Maybe a relationship ends because, even though we knew we needed to reconnect, life was too hectic and we ignored the voice of intuition. Or our children freeze us out because we are too busy with other things to create quality time. This can happen in business, family, financially, with our health, or any area that affects our lives.

We are always receiving guidance, but it is up to us to listen or to ignore it and suffer the consequences. Why is it so hard to listen and follow this inner knowing? We are creatures of habit, and it's easier to make excuses than to honor the sacred space inside that knows better.

This habit of listening is something I'm learning to honor more and more as I get older. I now realize this inner knowing is a priceless gift. No one has the answers for you. It may take courage to change, but there is often hidden wisdom to guide us.

Can you think of a time when you were dating someone, buying something, or saying yes to something only to have it not work out and you looked back and said, "I knew it!"? Our intuition never lies to us; its sole purpose is to help us live out our truth. The problem is that many of us have learned how to deny our truth to keep the peace, please another, or myriad other excuses. This is not an area I have mastered, but it is an area I'm always working on and believe is worth taking the time to check into.

The one thing I ask for on a daily basis is for help and guidance in living my truth. Being human, we are sometimes unsure of what our truth even is. You've probably heard, "The truth will set you free." I believe that's a valid statement. But knowing how to listen to our truth takes practice. Practice will unlock the door to hearing what our souls know. Although it takes time to get familiar with this, the voice inside is well worth listening to because of its truthful accuracy.

One way I've found helpful to connect to my truth is by getting still. Our lives seem to crave constant stimulation, and while there is absolutely a time to grind, there is also a part of being human that calls for the opposite.

The habit of listening requires desire. It also requires making time to do this on a regular basis. I've found that mornings are best, before the day has its way with you. Having daily quiet time may feel weird at first if you're not used to it, but it can become your most sacred time of the day.

My morning quiet routine is a bit impromptu in the sense that I just go with what feels right. The one thing that never changes is breathing deeply. Inhale deep into your belly, letting it expand. Exhale through your nose, letting your belly deflate. Other than that, go with what feels right to you. It could be writing a little, reading something inspirational, or just sitting and breathing with your eyes closed. Whatever gets you to a place of stillness is what works best.

Ask to hear whatever is most beneficial for you to know. It can be about your day in general, or maybe something specific that's in your heart to ask. I usually place one hand over my heart and one over my solar plexus, then just listen to what comes up. Placing my hands feels like my invitation for my heart and intuition to speak. Being quiet is where you can hear what your truth says.

Of many self-care practices, this is one of my favorites because so much comes up in life, and there are times when *only you* will know what's best for you. Listening to others is beneficial, as long as they are qualified, but you must learn how to consult with your truth in order to intentionally set out to be the best version of yourself.

I remember many years ago, when I started my Pilates and coaching business, a person very dear to me told me that I wouldn't make it and it would be smarter to go out and get a nine-to-five. This person felt like family, and it almost felt as if I was betraying a tribe member who was giving sound and safe advice. What I see now is that person was speaking their truth—*it just didn't happen to be mine.*

You need to know your truth because we all come to crossroads. When you're at a crossroad, people just love to share their opinions and give advice. **It's OK to realize that what is true for one person doesn't mean it's right for you.** Don't get me wrong, I believe in seeking out advice from well-qualified people, but you must learn to hear what you heart and intuition have to say and be ready to honor that.

2. Be Courageous

E.E. Cummings said, "It takes courage to grow up and become who you really are." I couldn't agree more. Especially when listening to your intuition means facing your fears. To be perfectly honest, some of the most challenging times in my life have been times when listening to and following my intuition went against much of what I'd been taught to do to stay *safe*. Sometimes I even questioned if going with my intuition would be the wrong move, because it has meant leaving people, places, and situations that still had some beneficial aspect.

You can make a mistake, but you must be courageous to follow your heart and find out for yourself. Often, even in the face of fear, once you pull the trigger and make the decision to follow your heart, an immediate relief follows.

Holding onto things that you've outgrown can feel like you're betraying some part of the past. These feelings can raise fears and make you want to avoid making any decision at all. Staying stuck in limbo is definitely not the place you will grow into your maximum potential. You must allow yourself to venture into the unknown, when that's where your heart is calling you. What you'll discover *there* is meant to be part of *your path and journey.*

The truth is that you are not going to be perfect and you will make mistakes. The other truth is that both of these facts are essential in becoming the best version of you.

There is something exhilarating in unapologetically following your heart and intuition and living your life 100 percent to your maximum potential. You will be amazed at what you will find when you take one step at a time toward whatever your intuition is calling to you.

You may be inclined to think that you need to have every detail figured out before you take a step toward your dreams, but I've seldom found that success works like that. Part of the mystery is finding out what you're capable of. Many times, things present themselves only after we've taken a leap of faith toward our heart's desire.

Not only can life become extremely exciting and rewarding, but we begin to realize that we are capable of so much more than we dared believe is possible. When you dare to be courageous is when the miracles, people, and opportunities show up. When you let fear rule your life, you sit on the sidelines bored, complaining, and not living a satisfying life.

Being courageous is a choice. Sometimes when I've felt afraid, I imagine someone who embodies courage walking next to me and giving me guidance. Often, it'd be Oprah or Gabrielle Bernstein. Just imagining a strong sister by my side would instantly make me feel better. Use this method whenever fear crops up.

3. Release Judgment

You may be wondering, "What does releasing judgment have to do with listening to my intuition?" A lot, actually. Being able to hear your inner guidance can be impossible if you're harboring judgmental thoughts about yourself or others.

In order to hear my intuition, I had to understand just how vital releasing judgment is. This lesson came through a rather humbling experience. Having no awareness as to why, there was a time I found it nearly impossible to hear my intuition. I felt blocked. Wanting to understand what was at the root of how I felt, I sat down to meditate. I asked God to give me the miracle of changing my mind by showing me what was creating this block. As always, ask and you shall receive!

What came through was that my judgments were blocking me from feeling good. The judgment I felt toward others, even if it was only dished out in my inner thoughts, had a boomerang effect. Whatever judgments I had toward others was reflected on myself. This created guilt and condemnation. Realizing that judgment held me captive, I began to understand how forgiveness was the way out of feeling blocked and limited. I then felt led to make a list of all the people I had been holding judgments against. Admitting the honest truth felt humbling. I'm thankful that it meant more to hear my inner guidance than keep my ego satisfied.

It was not easy to make this list, but it was easy to know who went on it. At the bottom, I also added myself. For each person on the list, the first thing I did was imagine they were sitting across the table from me and looking into my eyes. I said their name and then said, "I forgive you. I bless you. I release you."

The next part was going back over the list again, this time to thank each person for three things. This part felt really good because I realized I'm capable of shifting my thoughts to look at the good of a person, just as easily as I can judge them. Being on the list myself also made me realize that I can forgive myself when I mess up.

This exercise taught me that judgment is like snapping a picture of a person, and then using that one extremely limited view to judge an entire person. All judgment comes from the ego, which separates and attacks. What we need to realize is that we also judge ourselves when we judge others. If others can be vulnerable to our attacks, then so can we. It is a place that fear enters and separates us from the love we truly seek.

Releasing judgment means releasing what is blocking us from our greater good. Because we project judgments outward, we can often be completely unaware that we're doing it. Considering that judgment is such strong, icky energetic stuff is reason enough to practice forgiving. Doing this daily will help train your focus to intentionally choose to see the good in others. Choosing to see the good in others is a wise choice, since it's the same mirror you'll be using to see yourself.

4. Trust Yourself

Trusting yourself is essential to following your intuition. Many people I've coached over the years have revealed an inability to trust and follow their intuition. This is often a result of trusting what other people think more than trusting their own inherit worth and believing they deserve to happily pursue their own path. People often continue to believe lies about their abilities and potential, because of what someone told them years ago. Growing up, we are vulnerable to criticisms and other's opinions. We may shrink in areas that we've been told we aren't good enough or that we don't have what it takes to do or be something. You may have been drawn to a particular thing, activity, form of self-expression, art, writing, hobby, or career, but stopped believing it was possible for you after hearing discouraging words or ridicule. This is often the case when people settle for an unsatisfying life because they don't believe they are worthy of more. Many people even feel guilty about it. They've bought into the idea that they're doomed to stay stuck. This is a lie. You only stay stuck if you don't choose to change.

Trusting yourself means that you can trust yourself to make the changes necessary to raise your standards and feel better in *any* area of your life. Living an unsatisfactory life will eventually lead you to become sick and tired of the way you feel, until you finally make a change.

When you can trust your heart and intuition, you'll have access to a form of guidance. There is a universal Source that speaks to us in the stillness. When I get still to listen, I receive guidance through an intuitive channel. It's not like I hear an audible voice, but when I ask questions and seek answers, my intuition opens and I'm able to hear the answers I seek. When you intentionally invite the truth to be revealed, it will. This guidance is a form of wisdom that loves you and wants you to be happy.

Sometimes, when I've felt unsure of my accuracy in perceiving a situation (since we all base the meaning we give to anything on the past) and I don't trust myself because I feel unclear, I'll ask for the miracle of changing my perception and seeing clearly. When you aren't sure of how you feel about something and therefore don't trust yourself, it's the perfect time to get still and ask for clarity. Sometimes your clarity doesn't come right away, but if you continue to be patient and continue asking, it will come.

Sometimes our answers come in surprising ways, but if you ask you will receive. Often, I've had specific things answered in dreams that revealed what I needed to know.

5. Schedule It In!

This may sound like a strange method to listening, but it's one of the most productive ways to make sure you actually do it! Life is busy, and while that's OK, it's also important to make time for your most important priority: YOU! There are probably many people in your life who rely on you and expect much from you in terms of time and energy, but you can only give the best of yourself if you take care of you first!

Even if you start small, with ten minutes in the morning to get still and check in with your heart and intuition, it will become time you look forward to because it sets the tone for your whole day. I know that some people may think this is woo-woo, but I'm not into woo-woo at all. What I am into is getting results to be the best version of myself.

Starting the day by getting up just in time to jump full speed into the day's business just isn't the same as having a little bit of quiet time to check in with yourself. It's a time to address anything going on inside you. There are so many ways to get centered, including meditating, writing, reading something inspiring, visualizing how well your day will go, and maybe even some EFT (emotional freedom technique). All of these practices help you get aligned so you can listen to your intuition. They also help you create the sacred space that will allow anything you need to ask, know, or receive to come through. Sometimes I look at my daily morning quiet time as my own personal therapy session. This time is the safest place to look at anything you want or need to, work through your stuff, and get the best answers.

When you listen to Source's guidance, life changes. It shifts from thinking you've got to manage all on your own to experiencing gratitude and knowing there is truly a higher power available to you 24/7. Listening to your heart and intuition is like a GPS that guides you whenever you are open to asking and receiving. It's simple, but it does take practice. Like any relationship, you want to spend time getting to know the deeper aspects of what your heart and soul yearns for. The best gift you can give yourself is *your time* to listen to your intuition on a daily basis. Schedule it in, and make it an appointment that you protect!

LESSON 6 ASSIGNMENT

1. Take ten minutes when you can be alone, quiet, and uninterrupted and sit comfortably with your eyes closed. Place your right hand over your heart and your left on your solar plexus (just below the center of your chest). Simply breathe and invite in whatever your heart and intuition want to say to you. You can bring up an area or ask for guidance about some specific situation. Take your time and relax. Allow whatever comes through to be heard without interference. Sometimes you'll want to stay here longer, but whatever feels right to you is right.

2. Write down what you experienced. Sometimes insights may come right away or they may take a while, depending on how tuned-in you are with your truth.

3. Thank and appreciate your truth no matter what it is.

4. For an optimal relationship with your inner guidance system, schedule time every morning to check in with whatever is going on in your life. Here you will always find the answers to your soul's path.

7 THE LESSON OF LIVING FROM THE END

I held a moment in my hand, brilliant as a star, fragile as a flower, a tiny sliver of one hour. I dropped it carelessly, Ah! I didn't know, I held opportunity.

—Hazel Lee

This is perhaps one of the most important practices I've made a regular part of my life, with nothing less than amazing results. It's a simple gift of imagination that most of us used as kids but never realized it was a gift at all. As adults, we're often told to look at "reality" when reality comes down to how we perceive it and react to it. More often than not, *reality* leaves us with a sense of powerlessness. This happens because when we're constantly reacting to what we see/hear/witness…we forget to go within… or that it's even an option in this fast-paced world. Yet going within is exactly how to tap back into your power, as well as create the much-needed changes in your own biochemistry.

How this works is easy. This was taught to me years ago by accident when I prayed for a new place to live. It wasn't that my apartment was bad, but the other apartments were so very close to mine that I didn't even have a view of the sky and it felt very depressing. So one night after I put my daughter to bed, I asked for guidance and it was as if something told me to go sit outside, on my little stoop under the awning. It was dark, and I sat on the steps and closed my eyes. Again, this inner prompting (God, the Source, Universal Energy, or whatever you call this Higher Power) told me to envision the place I'd like to live. Not only to envision it, but to truly *feel it.* So I took my time and thought of what it felt like when I'd walk in the door, the colors and the layout, the view of the sky and light beaming in, and all the details from room to room. I allowed my whole mind, body, and emotions to pretend as if I was actually experiencing this.

To my surprise, I got excited going through this process. After about twenty minutes, I went in and looked at the paper. I called about an apartment listed in the paper but I got a voicemail, so I hung up. About a half-hour later, I got a call from the Realtor saying that he saw he missed a call. After explaining that I'd called about the apartment, we set up a time to meet the next day. To my surprise, this place felt as if it had come right out of my visualization. It was set on a forty-acre Christmas tree farm with all that I envisioned and more. The Realtor said that I was the first to see it, and this apartment became the next place I'd live for a few years.

Merriam-Webster's dictionary defines living as "exhibiting the life or motion of nature," the word "from" is "used as a function word to indicate the starting or focal point of an activity" and the word "end" as "the extreme or last part."

Living from the end means going forward in your mind's eye, embracing every conceivable shape and form, and feeling your goal as if it's already been achieved. When you come back into your present reality, you'll behave and live as if your goal *has already been achieved.*

The experience of visualizing from the end sets the tone for how things will go. The truth is, you've already been there before it happens. If you visualize daily, living from the end becomes such a familiar place that when you arrive at whatever the scene is in real life, it's truly as if you'd already been there. Many sports coaches teach their players how to visualize practicing and winning, with amazing results. Doesn't the real game of your life deserve nothing less?

FIVE QUESTIONS TO IDENTIFY A LACK OF LIVING FROM THE END

1. Do you feel nothing exciting when you wake up?
2. Do you feel how you want to feel each day?
3. Are you making daily progress toward your goals and dreams?
4. Is your focus scattered?
5. Have you lost peace and become fearful?

There's nothing wrong with wherever you're at right now in your journey. No one's perfect and no one ever will be. It's not about being perfect, but it is about becoming the best version of YOU! So let's keep moving forward toward whatever inspires you to move closer to that version of yourself now.

FIVE METHODS TO LIVE FROM THE END

1. Visualize Daily

Living from the end is a practice of imagination, faith, and feeling. To truly change your life, I highly recommend visualizing on a daily basis. Simply close your eyes and imagine being, doing, or having whatever is in your soul that will bring you closer to the best version of yourself. If you're a visual person, this will be easier, but either way it's worth cultivating. This is one area where you can have anything your heart desires *without limits*. Give yourself *fully* to the experience. Feel it with every one of your senses. What does it look like? How does it taste? What are the smells around you? What are you hearing? How does it feel to touch? How do your heart and soul feel? It should feel satisfying and fulfilling in every way. Look at the details of what your experiencing. What does the scenery look like? What are you wearing? Who are the people with you? Take your time. Allow whatever you see/feel/smell/touch/hear to add to the reality of your experience, as if you're actually living from here *right now.*

When you do this over and over, you'll begin to feel familiar and comfortable. Being, doing, and having *all starts with an idea* of what it looks and feels like. You must *see in your mind's eye* what is possible if you ever intend for this to become your reality. If you can't see it, it will be nearly impossible to believe you can achieve it. Practicing this will take some time.

Whatever time you invest in visualizing your future is worth it. This is a very powerful way to become vibrationally aligned and connected on a deeper level to living your best self.

Once your visualization session is over, let it go into the ether and have faith that you are setting into motion an amazing new reality. It's important to feel good while visualizing, and it's equally important to release attachment to it once the daily session is over.

2. Cultivate Emotion

To truly activate the art of living from the end, it must be mixed with genuine emotion. Many times, we base our emotions solely on what is happening externally. Part of creating your life intentionally is realizing you can cultivate your emotions through visualization.

Emotions drive how you feel about everything. Many times, you may not even be aware of them, or you may even suppress them. It's important to realize that the decisions you make are primarily emotionally based. That's why companies spend so much money on advertising. They understand that if their marketing can make you *feel* happy, you'll associate that feeling with their product. This is a huge reason why you've got to think about what you're thinking about!

When you cultivate how to see your *now* you'll realize that the emotions you choose play a crucial factor in sustaining this vision. You must learn to constantly focus on the best version of yourself in your future/now state.

Instead of letting other people, places, and things take charge of how you feel, take control of your emotions by becoming aware of what you're focusing on. If there's an area you want to change, you must look to see if you've been dwelling on past failures. If you focus on unpleasant past situations, it will bring fear, sadness, disgust, or other negative emotions. These emotions keep you powerless.

Choosing to visualize and create emotion intentionally will recondition your mind to understand its role as creator. You can't *not* feel emotions. They are part of the human experience. Consciously choosing your emotions is consciously choosing the kind of life experience you will have. The choice is always yours.

One way to choose your emotion is by feeling the way you do while visualizing, then taking how you feel *after from* your visualization and *live inside that emotion now.* This means that if you feel very joyful while visualizing the most loving relationship with the person of your dreams, bring the feeling of joy with you when you come out of your visualization. Become merged with joy. Smile and act as you would if this visualization were your current reality. Emotion is so strong that you want to linger in the good ones for as long as you can! This requires a bit of vulnerability. The reason is when you close your eyes and imagine what you desire, you must *let go.* You must let go of your current experience, so you can truly feel how wonderful it will be to reach your goals and live your dreams.

Letting go is the gap where your future is created. Whether it's living in a healthy body, being in a relationship with the person of your dreams, living in your dream home, starting a business, being sure and confident, being financially independent, being the best athlete you can be, traveling to places you've never been, or *anything* that would enhance your life for the better…you must let go and allow yourself to *sink deeply into the emotion* that accompanies your future reality. Allow yourself to step into that picture and feel how incredible creating your life can be. Own your best self with every fiber of your being, and choose this way of seeing yourself, day in and day out.

If you've never thought of choosing your emotions intentionally, it may seem impossible. What's possible, however, is to *train your focus toward what you do want,* instead of what you don't. Training your focus does not come naturally for most people, because we've grown accustomed to the constant bombardment of stimulation. Unending interruptions with notifications, phone calls, texts, emails, and social media have made multitasking seem like a good thing. What gets lost among this untrained way of using your attention is the inability to focus on creating your life versus reacting to it.

Learning to use the "Do not disturb" button on my phone has been a lifesaver whenever I need to focus on something (like writing this book)! It isn't the norm, but you can shut off interruptions. This is critical so your focus can be maximized.

When it becomes a habit to care about how you feel, you will see the link between what you focus your attention on and your emotional state. This is key to understanding that the quality of your life can be changed dramatically by scanning where you've been placing your attention, and deciding if this is what you want to continue feeling. Believe that you can always change if you choose.

3. Prepare Yourself

Feel good that what you're visualizing and creating emotion towards *is* coming. Do whatever you can do every day, no matter how small, to advance your personal development into being the person who has already attained your desired outcome. It's important to allow the energy that you feel during your visualization to prompt some action each day so you're ready and able to handle your goal once it's achieved. Preparation is a vital element because you get what you prepare for.

Learn to pair your visualizations with regular preparation. An example of this is when I get ready for a speaking engagement. First, I visualize it going well and leaving the building smiling after giving the audience value they can take into their own lives. I see myself as confident, having great energy, dressed well, being aligned and well prepared, and allowing the energy of the Universe to flow through me while delivering my presentation. Along with this, I prepare my materials, know my outline and talk, eat well, have my clothes laid out, get enough sleep, stay hydrated, work out, and give myself plenty of time to get to where I'm going. All this preparation is to ensure I've done my part for a smooth and successful day. There are many things that are out of my control, but I can be in control of how I prepare myself.

There is a great word of advice I can mention here: you must learn to balance drive *with* patience. Being driven is a beautiful gift that will open many doors and opportunities. But being patient is also necessary because great things take time. The more you can learn to lean into both drive and patience, the more you can enjoy the journey toward achieving your desired result.

Using visualization while making daily progress in preparing yourself to be the person who mentally, physically, and emotionally *can handle* what you're hoping to change and attain is a key to success. There is always more to learn and ways to grow as you work toward becoming the best version of yourself. An example is someone who wants to change their body by losing weight and getting fit. While *the act of visualizing* will allow you to imagine feeling awesome in a healthy body, and how it would change your life in so many ways for the better, visualization is not enough by itself. Visualization *must* be combined with daily action steps to make it a reality.

One good way to build momentum is to realize that *daily action steps are the key.* Progress creates confidence that you can actually do it! Daily progress will make you feel good. Like compound interest, it grows. Momentum will build, and you'll begin to realize that you truly can affect change toward your intention!

Remember that you are building your world from the inside out instead of feeling powerless to affect only what you can see and touch.

4. Time Management

We all have twenty-four hours in a day, and how we use this time ultimately determines whether we get to live the best version of ourselves. When I first realized that living the best version of myself was going to change from a "could" to a "must," I came face to face with my lack of time management. When you're raising your standards, going for your heart's desire and making changes to better your life, you need to look at your time in a new way. Before getting serious about reaching my goals, I'd drift this way or that, doing whatever got my attention, or even worse, doing little or nothing. I was a master at distracting myself from whatever I didn't feel like dealing with. I'm not proud to admit it, but this is how it was for years. *Until* I got serious that I wanted more. I knew that living a more satisfying and fulfilling life meant I needed to change how I managed my time.

Visualizing, creating the emotion to carry into your day, and preparing yourself with daily action steps will quickly reveal the lesson that everyone who goes for great must encounter. Why is time management so important? Do you have extra hours lying around to devote to new practices to develop and prepare yourself? Probably not. Everyone's busy, and sometimes what we already have going on feels like too much, never mind adding new things that won't give immediate gratification.

When you introduce something new to your life, it will eventually create pressure. It may be pressure in the form of getting up earlier and wanting to stay in bed, or resistance from people in your life who are used to having you available at a certain time, and even your own discomfort in stretching past your comfort zone. The forms of pressure are endless. Getting good at boundaries and limits will help immensely. With other people especially, and even with yourself sometimes, you must learn to say no in order to say *yes* to living the best version of yourself.

I use the word "policy" to communicate a boundary. An example of this is:

> "It's my policy not overextend myself when my schedule is full. Thank
> you for the invitation, and if anything changes I'll let you know, but
> right now I need to decline [fill in the blank]."

To myself I'd even say, "It's my policy to be the best that I can be, so no matter what that means I need to do, I'm committed to doing whatever it takes."

Learning how to manage your time will help you reach your goals and dreams. It won't happen unless you make it happen, so make sure you know how you're honestly spending your time. Make the adjustments that need to made in order to work on yourself every day. Living from the end means setting a time of day to visualize, intentionally cultivate the emotion you choose to live from, and taking daily steps towards your desired outcome. If you do this consistently, you'll begin to feel closer to attaining your goal.

5. Use Pressure to Expand

My daughter and I have pet ball pythons. One of my favorites, Bud, happened to escape one night after I forgot to put the clamps on the lid of his tank. In the morning, I noticed that his hide (a piece of hollowed wood where he hides) was moved to one side of his tank and one of the clamps had fallen to the floor. Not thinking much, I picked up the clamp and set it next to his tank. Shortly after, I went to say my usual good morning to Bud. After looking around his tank, I realized he'd escaped. My heart sank.

The most troubling part was there was a vent next to the clamp on the ground. We emptied closets, looked in shoes, and checked underneath everything, but could not find Bud. Eventually my daughter and her friends, along with my boyfriend and his kids, all came over in search of Bud. No one could find him.

Working from home, Bud was my companion most days while I worked at my desk or read. For two days I didn't even eat. My heart felt heavy. Days went by, and although I even dreamt of finding Bud, I worried that the vent had literally been his downfall. The crazy part was, I didn't think he even could escape. But I realized he must have used all his pressure to push against his hide and open the lid. He was obviously determined to get out.

One morning, about a week after Bud escaped, I sat in meditation and asked my inner guide to show me a new way to see the situation. What came filled me with a new sense of understanding about using our own pressure to escape our own cages. Here's what came from my automatic writing after my meditation that morning:

> Leaving the cage of what is no longer comfortable happens because you were made for more. Use the pressure inside of you to open the lid of your container. The container you've created can be opened and escaped from when the pressure inside you becomes great enough. You may leave your container and others will wonder where you went. You may be MIA for a while, like Bud. You may emerge back on the scene once you've explored other aspects that your soul has been craving. This exploratory time is necessary to lead you to other

points of view that you wouldn't have experienced had you never left your cage...it simply isn't possible.

Getting out of whatever you see as limiting your life is like living in the basement until deciding one day to head out to the penthouse to see what life looks like from there. Nothing had actually changed except the perspective from which you were able to see. True seeing is being able to change perspective from our limiting viewpoint. A whole new world opens up once we change how we look at things.

Often, we simply need to leave the cage of our minds and seek higher ground to see a thing. The higher ground is often revealed in stillness and upon the asking. Asking for a change in perspective is a powerful prayer because it's the opening necessary for an inspired thought or idea to come through. These moments are available to us all the time. It's only when we forget to ask that we stay stuck in the cage of our own making.

I've always marveled at how small things seem when lifting off in an airplane. I feel like we all look like little ants. When life gets overwhelming, I've often thought of this. It's comforting to realize that my point of view is small in comparison to the whole. It's comforting because I know we all have access to a bigger picture through asking.

When I look at something that's bothering me, I know I'm seeing it from my small perspective. I know when this happens because I feel it. Peace leaves my body, and I feel fearful. This is the exact time I've learned to ask for the miracle of a change in perspective and another way of seeing a situation.

Part of living from the end is allowing our souls to guide our earthly journeys. What we see is determined by where we stand in our minds. Never be afraid to let go of limiting beliefs in areas where you've felt confined for far too long. You are meant to live your life as the best version of yourself, and the only thing stopping you is you. To get out of your own way, you'll have to be willing to see things differently. This might seem scary because our thought systems can be strong when it comes to certain things. We believe we can or can't do something based on how we look at things. Don't be afraid to ask your inner guide to give you the miracle of changing your mind. Once you get used to living this way, you won't cling so tightly to your one way of seeing things. A whole new world opens when you use the pressure inside that wants more out of life to open the lid to the container of your mind.

As a side note, over two weeks later, Bud did eventually appear. Late night during a lightning storm, I went into my office to shut down my computer and lo and behold, there was Bud on my dog Lily's bed. Never have I forgotten those clamps again!

WRAP UP

It's worth mentioning that living from the end is a powerful tool to use in *every* area of your life. Even in difficult or challenging situations, you can choose to see from the end. It will make you a better person with more character, patience, understanding, wisdom, knowledge, and priceless experience that will serve you moving forward.

There is always a choice in how you see yourself. Sometimes there's resistance to this truth, but it's only because it requires you to use your mind in a way that switches you back to your birthright as a creator.

For so long you've been trained by mass consciousness to embrace reasons you should be fearful, worry, and talk about everything that is wrong in your life and in the world. The majority of reaction-based people live their lives from a victim mindset. This isn't about judgment—it's about waking up to your true identity as a powerful creator. Living from the end is a way to direct your mind and life in a new way. When you're looking past whatever exists today and focusing in a solution-oriented way, you step into the truth of what you came here to do. Expand and create.

It's always up to you how you respond to life and who you choose to become. Again, the goal is to be the best version of yourself and use daily practices and tools, such as living from the end through visualization, that put you back in the driver's seat.

You will be disappointed or hurt by something or someone at some point. You don't want to be stuck in the past, reliving your woes long after the actual event is over and unable to move on. Living from the end with a new outcome is a powerful way to see yourself in a more confident, loving, and wise way. As you think, so shall you be…always.

LESSON 7 ASSIGNMENT

1. Sit comfortably where you won't be disturbed for at least fifteen minutes. Relax and close your eyes. Allow your mind to go forward to the time when you have achieved your goal/ideal outcome. In your mind's eye, you are living this out *now*. Really allow yourself to be emerged in the experience of what your life looks and feels like. Where are you living? Who are you with? What are you wearing? How are you spending your time? Take your time and try to capture the feeling. Lean into this emotion as much as you can. Let your five senses wrap around this emotion as you experience living at the most satisfying and fulfilling level imaginable. What would you feel, smell, hear, touch, taste? Let yourself imagine each detail as if slowly enjoying each morsel of the experience. Stay as long as you like. When it's time to end your visualization, ask the emotion you felt in the visualization to spend the day with you. Once you open your eyes, know that this emotion is alive inside of you now.

2. Write down what you just experienced.

THE LESSON OF THE F WORD

True forgiveness is when you can say, "Thank you for that experience."

—Oprah Winfrey

Being the best version of yourself is simply going to demand more than a couple Fs! Specifically, the F I'm referring to is the beautiful muscle of forgiveness. To harbor negativity toward others or, even more importantly, yourself is far too great a price to pay for your joy, peace of mind, and chance at living the best version of you.

It's crazy that some folks hold onto all kind of negative stories and replay them constantly without giving thought to the natural laws of the Universe. What comes up must come down. As within, so without. What you give comes back to you. These are spiritual laws that, if understood, make you want to get rid of anything inside you that creates ill will. That's probably a Pollyanna thing to say in the world we live in today, but as creators we still create our own worlds through our thoughts and the stories we tell ourselves. These stories shape not only our lives but also attract or repel the experiences that we allow into them.

Years ago, I had some much-needed growing up to do. I would hold onto a perceived "wrong" and tell the story with pride, as if *of course* I was right to feel offended and hurt. Maybe it was true and maybe not. It all comes down to perception. There are so many sides to every story. Every person holds within them not only their specific wiring but also how they were raised, their own beliefs about how things should be and about themselves, and a plethora of other constantly changing factors. When analyzing things from other perspectives, it became unmistakably clear there was no way I was truly qualified to judge another.

Merriam-Webster's dictionary defines forgiveness as "to cease to feel resentment against (an offender)."

First, I had to get honest about my own shortcomings, mistakes, and my own poor choices and decisions. Then I had to be able to forgive, love, and unconditionally accept myself anyway. This took years of learning to see myself beyond the limited version of who I was on the outside. I was soon able to see myself as the unlimited being that I am—and that YOU ARE. It isn't conceited to say this because we are powerful, beautiful, creative beings who, by our divine birthright, were created this way. Every single thing you can see was a thought, an idea, first. We are sometimes limited in seeing ourselves as we've been truly designed because of family, religious, social, cultural and generational conditioning. Forgive that too, or it'll only hold you back.

Forgiving is about releasing yourself and anyone else from preventing you from being the best version of yourself. Some people choose to hold onto the past and events that have been painful, believing it's holy to be a martyr. I think the worst travesty is not living full-out and then dying without ever seeing your potential. Forgiveness sets you free.

If there's someone you feel you can't forgive, even yourself, it may be time to visualize an open, honest, and loving conversation with this person. It may or not be possible if they're not still living, but you can visualize it in your mind's eye. It's important to be genuine and sincere about doing the best you possibly can to release toxic feelings. A clear conscience is a priceless thing indeed, and once again, is your CHOICE. If you choose to forgive, you can. If you choose to love and accept yourself unconditionally, you can. If you choose to believe people are doing the best they can for their level of understanding, you can. This sets you up to be president and CEO of your life, and that means you're in charge—in other words, you have freedom.

FIVE QUESTIONS TO IDENTIFY A LACK OF FORGIVENESS

1. Do you often feel a negative hit in your gut when you think about someone?
2. Does thinking about this person actually make you feel ill?
3. Do you gossip about him/her without confronting them directly?
4. Do you feel you have anything in common with this person?
5. Do you think this person added value to your life?

What few people want to admit is that we've all resented things people have done to us, that didn't make us feel good. Sometimes we've suffered physical, mental, or emotional abuse. We have places that are tender and can be easily triggered because of what you've experienced. But if you don't forgive yourself, these very places inside of you can also sabotage you.

This happens because eventually triggers will come up. If you haven't forgiven, the trigger can pull you in the opposite direction of being the best version of you. This can be a slippery slope. The contrast between how you *want* to be and how you *feel inside* may be so great that you think you *can't* become the best version of yourself. This feeling has been the downfall of many people. Once your attention is focused on resentment, you can't be at peace. Instead, you may cope by focusing on anything outside of yourself. You retell the same old story about how it wasn't right (to anyone who'll listen), get depressed, ask why your life's a mess, and distract yourself with food, drugs, sex, working, shopping, or any other addiction.

There is a way past all these self-defeating ways of dealing with resentment, and that's through forgiveness.

FIVE METHODS TO FORGIVENESS

1. Clean House

There's a story I share with my clients about the invisible emotions inside us. It's so easy to live in a world where you operate only based on what you *see* and ignore what you don't. This is a huge obstacle to living as the best version of you.

This is how I look at it: negative emotions are like burglars. Would you let a burglar rob and steal from you and let them live in your home? Would you tip-toe around this burglar? Would you give the burglar your bed while you sleep on the floor? Would you let this burglar dirty your entire home while you walk around the mess? This is exactly what you're doing when you allow negative emotions to take root in your mind.

Most of us weren't taught to see our inner lives. The truth is, no matter how good we can make ourselves look on the outside, what we feel *inside* is actually paramount.

We all hear about people who we thought had their lives together and then a tragedy happens and we realize we had no idea what was going on within.

Until you begin to take your inner landscape seriously and take control of what takes root in your heart and mind, you will find yourself spending most of your time and energy reacting instead of creating your life. Cleaning house is just that: taking an honest look at the resentments and negative junk that take you away from feeling good and consume your time and energy.

A helpful way to gain clarity on exactly what is taking up space in your head is to write down a list of the things that bother you on a daily basis. You may be surprised that you resent things such as cleaning, feeling taken for granted at home or work, feeling lonely, or not having the kind of social life you crave. Or maybe you've been divorced and still see red at the injustices that followed. Maybe finances have you resentful, or it could be your body and how you've neglected it. Or you feel resentful that you never seem to have the time to do the things you'd rather be doing. As you can see, resentments can stem from myriad places. No matter what you find, getting honest about it is the first step.

Once you've finished your list, draw a box around it. On the outside of the box, write five things that make you feel *really good*. This could be your kids or pets, doing work that you love, being at the ocean, your freedom to reinvent yourself, a relationship or friendship…even your decision to become the best version of yourself.

Lastly, inside the box write, "Choosing to be right." Outside the box, write, "Choosing to be happy."

When you realize that what you look at ultimately becomes how you will feel, wouldn't you rather feel good?

Forgiving is simply an act of choosing to feel the best that you can, while letting go of what no longer serves you. No matter what's happened in the past, it only gets dragged into your *today* through your focus. Forgiving is one of the most loving choices you can make. You can't make anyone else happy, but it's your job to make yourself happy.

Forgiveness is like a key we forget we have. It lifts the burden of carrying heavy things that we aren't meant to carry. Forgive yourself, others, situations, the past, memories from childhood, your parents, the neighbors, and all the things.

The only thing you can control is what you do from this moment forward. Through forgiveness, release yourself from anything that weighs you down. Look at the wonderful things you're creating ahead and forgive the past. Let anything except this moment slip away like sand through your fingers. Release your attachments and find your freedom.

Life is not about being perfect—but having peace inside is your choice to make despite life's imperfections. Through forgiveness, this peace takes the place of the burglars in your mind.

2. Choose Health

Conflict doesn't just weight down the spirit, it can lead to physical health issues. Whether it's a simple spat with your spouse or a long-held resentment toward a family member or friend, unresolved conflict can go deeper than you may realize.

"There is an enormous physical burden to being hurt and disappointed," says Karen Swartz, MD, director of the Mood Disorders Adult Consultation Clinic at The John Hopkins Hospital. Chronic anger puts you into a fight-or-flight mode, which results in numerous changes in your heart rate, blood pressure, and immune response. Forgiveness, however, reduces stress, leading to improved health.

Stress doesn't only make us feel awful emotionally, says Jay Winner, MD, author of *Take the Stress Out of Your Life*, it can also exacerbate just about any health condition you can think of.

Studies have found many health problems related to stress. Stress seems to worsen or increase the risk of conditions like obesity, heart disease, depression, gastrointestinal problems, and even asthma.

Of course, stress is a part of life, but there is a difference in day-to-day stress and carrying resentments inside that literally eat away at your chance for peace and happiness. Many of us have been conditioned to believe that it's easier to carry around our hurts and injustices at the cost of our own health than to let the burdens go. Forgiveness offers you the chance out of this energy-draining hell. It is a choice you can make for yourself that has so many benefits. The best part, besides adding tremendous value toward living the best you, is that it's absolutely free!

According to the Mayo Clinic, forgiveness brings plenty of health benefits, including improved relationships, decreased anxiety and stress, lower blood pressure, a lowered risk of depression, and a stronger immune system and heart health. Letting go of negative emotions can have a remarkable impact on the body.

Choosing health means protecting it from anything that would take it from you. We understand this with our physical bodies, which is why we don't step into the street when cars are coming, try to eat healthy, and get enough sleep. But we also must choose health for our inner emotions. Forgiving doesn't mean forgetting or condoning the wrong committed against you. Forgiveness is for *you*! In your journey to become the best you, forgiveness is the most loving gift you can give yourself.

A recent study in the *Journal of Health Psychology* revealed that having the trait of forgiveness independently predicts positive mental and physical health. Researchers found that forgiveness protects against stress's negative effects on mental health. "We found that lifetime stress severity was unrelated to mental health for persons who were highest in forgiveness, significantly associated with poorer mental health for persons exhibiting moderate levels of forgiveness, and most strongly related to poorer mental health for participants exhibiting the lowest levels of forgiveness," they wrote.

To guard your health, be open to choosing peace and love as your inner companions. Think of forgiveness as maintenance for keeping these companions.

3. Seeing Your Mirror

The truth is, we are all mirrors for each other. It's only possible to see what you see in another because you have that element in yourself. You may disagree, but if you think about it, even the things that disgust you, or that you'd label as wrong, wouldn't even be in your awareness if there weren't those parts of yourself. That's why the more you judge and criticize others, the more you judge and criticize yourself. It's a vicious, mean, and hateful cycle. The good news is that the same rules apply in forgiveness. Forgiving others also applies to being able to forgive yourself.

Martin Luther King Jr. said, "We must develop and maintain the capacity to forgive. He who is devoid of the power to forgive is devoid of the power to love. There is some good in the worst of us, and some evil in the best of us. When we discover this, we are less prone to hate our enemies."

The truth is, when we realize we are all mirrors for each other, our reactions soften and the question can then be asked: "How can I learn from this?"

Understanding this can drastically alter how we react to the things that happen to us.

A long time ago, I learned a valuable lesson from someone I'd dated. Although he seemed to be a nice enough guy early on, I noticed he could be very distant. I expressed how important communication was to me. He'd admit he could do better. When I was with him, we got along for the most part. When I wasn't with him, it felt like I didn't even have a boyfriend.

Most of the time—wanting to *be nice*—I didn't say anything. But over time, suppressing my truth made me feel angry, guilty, and frustrated. This created a cycle inside my head, but I kept that in too. I'd silently feel my feelings, and then act like everything was fine when I'd see him. At the time, I thought I was being nice. Now I realize it was very unhealthy behavior. Many of us learned behaviors in our childhoods that no longer serve us as adults.

Continuing to feel unheard and unimportant, resentment began to fester. I continuously tried to go above and beyond to reach a deeper place of connection. I thought that would warm his coldness, and I'd feel closer to him. Despite my efforts, I began to feel we simply couldn't connect. I began distancing myself. I started avoiding his calls and texts. This began a passive aggressive cycle that neither of us talked about. When I did see him, we didn't talk about feelings at all. We pretty much acted like we had none. Neither of us ended up sharing much beyond surface stuff. We almost broke up several times.

The day came when I discovered that he wasn't being honest with me. He had lied to me a few times. When confronted, he actually made up three different stories about why he lied. I broke up with him. When I look back, it made no sense at the time. As always, I took it to meditation.

I bring this story up because using this practice of seeing another as your mirror offers a way out of staying stuck in judgment. It gives you the opportunity to ask how you could see yourself in the other person, and realizing a part of yourself in the situation.

Admitting to myself that I'd been passive aggressive and not spoken my truth helped me to see my part. The truth was, I wasn't satisfied. My decision to settle for less made me realize the resentment I'd projected outward was really directed at myself for not speaking up. I was angry at myself for staying in a relationship I didn't feel good about.

Instead of blaming him, I realized I was the one who needed to take responsibility for my own happiness. Also, despite how angry and resentful I felt, I still acted as if everything was OK. It made me face how I had chosen to continue this relationship, taking no action to remedy it. Acting powerless, I turned to denial instead of speaking my truth.

I had to remind myself that we're all doing the best we can for our level of awareness. At the time I could see this was as true for him as it was for me. Knowing this, I could forgive, because it was the only way to set us both free.

There is a lot of fear around speaking up in relationships. Many people grew up being taught that you're supposed to be quiet, nice, and not make waves. I avoided confrontation at all costs. It was such an internal battle for so long! I didn't speak up for fear of disapproval, rejection, or seeming needy. This form of suppressing my feelings led to guilt and shame.

Although I wasn't the one who technically lied, I felt like I hadn't been honest with myself. I lied to my truth by not speaking my truth and faking that I was OK with how things were. This experience taught me that I could see *he was me.* Everything that happened was a reflection I could either learn from or feel a victim to. This was the point of taking my power back. Choosing to see how he was mirroring back to me things I needed to work on in myself, I became thankful for this gift of inner sight.

I made the intentional choice to forgive him *and myself.* Instead of seeing this as a negative experience, I saw it as a great learning opportunity that could help me grow and be better. It was also a moment of self-realization as I became aware of a continuous pattern of not speaking up in my relationships. If there was something that bothered me, I'd avoid it, turn the conversation away from it, or deny it. Because I was open to seeing my role in how the relationship played out, I could begin changing this in myself.

For anyone who feels they're *too nice,* I highly recommend reading *Not Nice* by Dr. Aziz Gazipura. This book helped me to "stop pleasing people, staying silent and feeling guilty...and start speaking up, saying no, asking boldly, and unapologetically being yourself."

The reason to choose forgiveness and learn what you can from every situation you encounter is to save yourself from feeling powerless. When you feel like a victim to your past, you'll justify why you'd been wronged and can stay stuck in this story for years. It's a powerless place. Achieving forgiveness and leveraging your experience to your benefit is simply a matter of shifting your perception inward.

Ask yourself:

- Are you more or less powerful for keeping resentment stored in your body for weeks, months, years, or a lifetime?
- Are you more or less powerful for choosing to forgive so you can move on with your life?
- Are you more or less powerful for using every experience to see where you can improve, grow, and become an even better version of yourself?

Bernie Siegel wrote, "You can survive tough situations and even turn them to your advantage by acting as if you are the person you want to be. When you act like that person, you can become that person. The hard parts are deciding whom you want to become, being willing to rehearse until you become that person, and forgiving yourself until you do."

One tool I use to forgive pretty much everything and anything is called EFT, or emotional freedom technique, also known as tapping. It's a strong tool that involves tapping on various meridians on your body that help you release areas in which you feel blocked. Working on forgiveness can bring up some strong triggers, and being able to move past them is what makes EFT so effective. Since it's something you can do by yourself, it's perfect for feeling safe while handling topics that can be highly emotional. I highly recommend it! There are many great books on the subject such as *The Tapping Solution* by Nick Ortner. Also check out YouTube videos, or do a Google search to show you how it's done. It's an effective way to move past anything that's got you stuck.

4. Travel Light

As described by Emma Johnston in *Light vs. Darkness Archetype*, "Light usually suggests hope, renewal, or intellectual illumination; darkness implies the unknown, ignorance, or despair."

When we choose to travel light, we choose to live in love. We do this by cleansing our hearts and minds through forgiveness. With daily practice, this can become a habit. Committing to a daily practice is how you condition your mind so you no longer feel separate or attack others when they differ from you. Your ego has endless ways to justify attacking people who are different.

Traveling light also means foregoing the ego's natural tendency to find reasons for being offended and justifying resentment. Your mind either shows up in the light of love or hides in the shadows with fear. This is the real choice you are making. It's always the choice between love and fear.

Remember that what you give, you also receive. This will help you identify what you *really* want to share. When you respond with ego and cling to the darkest parts of your thought system, you remain in the dark and keep fear alive. Through forgiveness, you no longer have to be bogged down with the dark stuff that resentments are made of.

Any moment you realize you're feeling fear and aren't in the light, you can choose again. Simply ask your inner guide for the miracle of changing your mind to see love instead of fear. Asking is the way to receiving. You aren't alone in your journey. You have support all around you for the *asking*. Don't forget to ask!

"The eye is the lamp of the body; so then if your eye is clear, your whole body will be full of light." —Matthew 6:22

Your eyes are used to see, but it's easy to forget that we are constantly choosing what we're looking at. When you look at the light, despite whatever imperfections you may have looked upon before, you are choosing the light over darkness. Love over fear.

Choosing to travel light doesn't mean there's no darkness. It simply means you are choosing to be part of healing the darkness. When you forgive, you heal one piece of darkness at a time. Every time you release a brother from the chains you would have kept him bound in, you're doing healing work. You and your brother are one. We all are connected. What you do to another is equally what you are doing to yourself. It may not seem like this, because we've been so conditioned to project outward, but when you choose to travel and live in the light, you can't help but realize we've all hurt ourselves and others. Love is the antidote to every fear. Light is the home of love, and choosing to live in the light is choosing to live in love.

When you've let go of your resentments, peace can fill that space. Peace is light. Love is light. Being in alignment is light. Joy is light. The best version of you is light.

Committing to a daily practice of traveling light is powerful because its purpose is to lighten your spirit. Just like you take a daily shower to wash off the residue of the day, you also need to wash away the residues of spiritual resentment. You've probably experienced how easy it is to be triggered and resentful. It often happens without you realizing it, and suddenly you're twisted up inside over something that you just reacted to without thinking. Road rage, anyone? Knowing that resentments *do* happen means it comes down how you deal with them that determines whether you travel back to the light or stay in the dark.

Traveling light allows you to let go of anything that prevents joy. It's also the path of staying in alignment and hearing your intuition clearly. When you get stuck in resentments and forget to forgive, you inevitably get blocked. The flow of joy, love, and peace ceases. You don't always know what just happened, but you can *feel* it.

An easy way to practice forgiveness is simply to ask yourself every morning and every night: "Who do I need to forgive?"

It is that simple! When you ask, you shall receive. An open heart and mind are powerful allies in your goal of living the best you. You can always handle letting things go, because you don't want to carry things that weigh you down and pull you away from your greatest good. You'll never lose by forgiving. Be willing to let go of whatever isn't serving your heart and mind.

5. Say Thank-You

Saying thank you turns a situation completely around. When you say *thank you*, your mind will begin to search for ways it has benefitted from having the experience. Feeling that you've gained some value makes every situation a learning experience.

When you realize you've lost your peace or feel resentment directed toward someone or yourself, get in the habit of saying "thank you." It softens your energy. It opens you up to seeing other possibilities you can grow from. Learning through pain is unfortunately how many of us learn some of our most powerful lessons. It's easy to point the finger and feel justified at being the victim, but it will never bring you to fulfillment.

When I look back on some of the most painful times in my life, I realize that's when I experienced the most growth. Physically, mentally, and spiritually, we all experience disappointments that cause pain. As I write this, my daughter and her boyfriend just broke up. This was her first-kiss, first-love-in-middle-school kind of boyfriend. Nobody ever forgets their first crush/love. When it ends, it sears your heart and you don't know if you'll survive it.

As I hug her and try to be there for her, I realize it's still her pain and she must feel her way through it. Of course, as a teenager, emotions run high and it's natural to like some drama. I get it! I've been there, where my heart felt heavy and broken. Certain heartbreaks took years to get over, and over time I wondered if there was a better way to handle life's disappointments. It's one thing to be fourteen, experiencing your first heartbreak, but it's another to never consider a different way of handling disappointments.

When in the presence of pain, we still have a choice. Learning to say thank you is one option. It's a quicker way back to your happiness, joy, and peace of mind and heart. Saying thank you doesn't mean you are thankful for everything in the experience. It's meant to take away from whatever caused you pain and make it work for you instead of against you. It's about taking back your power. Saying thank you helps you realize how you benefitted. Getting value out of every experience is one way to stay out of victimhood and look for ways to learn and grow.

When my ex-boyfriend lied to me and I found out, I had been practicing saying thank you for so long that I was able to move on from that breakup with gratitude. It wasn't a fake gratitude, but a genuine appreciation for a) having found out, b) saving time, c) becoming clearer on my own level of self-respect, d) learning a lesson about always voicing my own truth, and e) knowing that I deserved better. I felt almost as if I was finally growing up when I decided I wasn't going to waste a day feeling sorry for myself. After all, there is still so much life happening around us! It's OK to take time to grieve, but it's a waste of time staying stuck in resentments and letting pain keep you from living your life.

Years ago, I would have held onto a resentment and wasted time going over it again and again. It was like running on a hamster wheel and never arriving anywhere. Sometimes we just don't know what we don't know.

Fortunately, the gift of getting older is having more perspective and realizing that time is precious. It's too precious to waste on anything that keeps us stuck and interferes with living as the best version of ourselves. It truly goes back to choosing whether you want to be happy or be right. I'm going with happy.

WRAP UP

Negative emotions drain you, ruin your health, make you ugly, waste your precious time and energy, and repel positive experiences and people. Forgiving yourself is about cleaning house and forgiving yourself for allowing it to have been such an unkempt mess for so long. It's about saying no more to things that pull you away from being the best version of yourself! It's a choice to upgrade your thinking and take a look at the emotions you hold toward yourself and others.

The F-it lesson is all about that. Find it. Forgive it. Move on. Period.

LESSON 8 ASSIGNMENT

1. Write down what or who you need to forgive. Be honest.

2. Write a letter or close your eyes and imagine having a conversation with this person, place, or thing, and acknowledge that in order to grow and become the best version of yourself, you are choosing to forgive and let go. It may not be easy, but if you ask (Universe/Source/God/Inner Guide) for help, trust that it will come. Be willing to let go of anything that no longer serves you in becoming the best you!

9 THE LESSON OF BOUNDARIES AND LIMITS

Boundary setting is really a huge part of time management.

—Jim Loehr

Your time and energy are priceless. Once you use them, they're gone. You don't want to waste them. The truth is, there are people, places, and things that either bring you forward in a positive way or they don't. Period. The part that needs to be understood and practiced are boundaries and limits. When you begin to make better choices, you're going to push up against some old patterns, creating discomfort. Boundaries and limits are meant to keep you in line with your best version of yourself by intentionally deciding what gets to stay in your life and what no longer has a seat at the table.

Merriam-Webster's dictionary defines boundary as "something that indicates or fixes a limit or extent." It defines limits as "the place enclosed within a boundary."

A specific moment comes to mind when I had to make a tough boundary and set a limit. It felt like my days were scheduled down to the minute. I loved and enjoyed most of what I was doing, but one particular project was feeling burdensome. The time needed for this project meant hours away from my daughter, and it took me away from living in a balanced way. Turning to my inner guide during meditation, I asked what I needed to do and instantly knew the answer. Ever feel like that? On the outside, this project looked like a great thing to be doing, but inside I wanted nothing more than to let it go! I knew I needed to put a boundary in place. To fix it, I scheduled what was *most important first* and then if there was anything left (which there often wasn't) it got a spot in my scheduler. It didn't take long to see that my heart just wasn't into this way of using my time and energy anymore. Eventually, I let go of the project. Relief, relief, relief!

Letting something go in order to make room for what makes us most at peace, can be surprising because many of us think we can do it all. I've always said that even the right thing at the wrong time is the wrong thing.

FIVE QUESTIONS TO IDENTIFY A LACK OF BOUNDARIES AND LIMITS

1. Do you constantly go, go, go until you have nothing left to give?
2. Do you have a hard time saying no?
3. Are you constantly feeling like you "should" be, do, or have something that you aren't being, doing, or having?
4. Do you feel resentful and angry that you have no time for yourself?
5. Are you mentally and physically exhausted?

FIVE METHODS TO CREATE BOUNDARIES AND LIMITS

1. Physically

Our bodies follow where our minds go. This can be great when we have good relationships, habits, eat well, get enough sleep, and feel good. But what happens when we lose our focus and begin to move in a direction that isn't good for us? This happens when you run yourself ragged, don't keep your promises to yourself, and break your commitment to your goals.

A client of mine had a goal to feel better by going on a morning walk. She decided to commit to walking five mornings a week. She kept her commitment for a couple days, and then one morning she was tired and pressed snooze. Another day she ended up checking her phone and got sidetracked until she realized almost an hour had passed and didn't have time to walk. When she told me about this, I could see she felt defeated. I suggested creating some new boundaries and limits around her goal. First, mark it down as a non-negotiable appointment. Second, limit anything else from getting her attention until *after* her walk. That meant no phone browsing, no pressing snooze, nothing that would become an excuse for not making progress. She realized she hadn't considered creating boundaries and limits. Once she got clear on what she needed to say no to, she realized that the act of saying no was actually the only way she could say yes to herself.

Throughout the years of studying wellness, I've come to understand that when stress reaches a certain point, bodies can break down, health issues can pop up, and people can fall into cycles of anxiety and depression. These things are extremely difficult to manage and may require medical attention. It's true that we're able to handle an incredible amount of *stuff*, but there is a tipping point. Sometimes we need to reassess if what we are doing is helping us or hurting us.

No matter what ails us, our bodies were designed to heal, given the proper conditions. Boundaries and limits are often necessary to create these proper conditions. After reading *You Can Heal Your Life* by Louise Hay, *Mind Over Medicine* by Lissa Rankin, *Allowing* by Holly Riley, *Crazy, Sexy Diet* by Kris Carr, and *Mind Body Prescription* by Dr. John Sarno, I saw how absolutely essential it is to *feel good*!

The opposite of feeling good puts strain on our bodies, which creates a stress response. This stress response is the singular, always-present factor that accompanies disease. Life has a way of gifting us with the opportunity to experience stressors. It's important to embrace, own, and take responsibility for your own well-being. As children, we naturally do what feels good because we were all born with that innate knowingness. As life surrounds us with chaos and distractions, we can lose sight of the importance of making "feeling good" a priority. Deadlines, to-do lists, telling ourselves we *should* do this or *should* do that, overextending, not saying no, depleting ourselves, overworking, and so on takes a whack at our minds and our bodies. If we are in a constant state of reaction and stress, our bodies are unable to relax and unable to heal. It isn't a noble thing to be proud of, to run yourself ragged and disrespect your body's need for rest, play, down-time, fun, and relaxation.

As an adult, it took me a long time to understand that loving yourself and practicing self-care are some of the most important things we can do for ourselves and everyone else in our lives. It's not selfish and it doesn't it take away from others. When you're feeling well, isn't that a better place to give to others from? The point is, you should be at the top of your to-do list.

Mark your calendar for regular time off, self-care practices, exercise, meal prep, dates with friends, outdoor adventures, exploration, and anything else that will help you balance doing with *being*. Take good care of yourself and know that you deserve your highest respect and love. It's your job to care for the incredible vessel you've been given to travel this earthly voyage in.

It's time to honor our physical selves with healthy boundaries and limits. You can learn to put your cell phone on Do Not Disturb and close the door when you're meditating/writing/exercising or doing anything else from which you don't want to be interrupted. Learn to say no once you've made a time commitment to yourself. Lean toward improving your life and dump the habit of overcommitting.

2. Sacred and Holey Buckets

Think of your focus as an investment in either a sacred or "holey" bucket. When you invest in a sacred bucket, it's a solid investment. These buckets may include spending time with your kids, family, friends, doing work you love, self-care practices, walks in nature, working out, meditating, or anything that invests positively in yourself now and for your future. When you invest in buckets with holes in the bottom, it's a waste of your sacred time and energy. These are "holey" buckets. If you find your attention is often in the past, it's time to create boundaries and limits in order to move forward.

To reclaim your power, notice where you're investing your time and energy and learn to redirect whenever you find you're investing in holey buckets. This redirection is a boundary to use when you realize your focus just went somewhere that isn't serving your best self.

One method of redirection is to write down positive aspects of what you can be doing now that will positively affect your future. These are the things that will make you feel good and move you forward. These are the things that raise your standards. You can turn your focus around when you decide that the quality of your life is directly reflected back to where you invest your focus. Any time you find you're investing in holey buckets, stop and write all the positive things you can think of that you can do NOW that will make you feel good and affect your future in a positive way. This can be as simple as working out or calling that friend who always boosts your spirits! It's a way to get your mind unhooked from the trail of thoughts that leads you somewhere that feels icky and pisses you off.

Another way to redirect your focus is what I call the "close the door on the past" technique. To move on, sometimes you literally need to close the door on what no longer serves you. Take a moment to be still and ask yourself: if you had to close the door to the past, how would your day be different? Envision yourself being the person you would be if you could only be present and focused on what was happening now. How would seeing yourself from this fresh perspective change the outcome of your day? What would happen if you had no choice but to be present and focused only on today? Try it right now. Pretend you're five feet above yourself, looking down and seeing yourself. You might be reading this, and you'll notice that. There's nothing else to notice when you're totally focused on right now.

You can switch into this observational mode whenever you find you're drifting someplace else. Every time you live in the past or your mind goes off somewhere that isn't serving you, you've left the present. Being present for your life, means being fully present in the moment you're living right now. Many of these moments together make up a satisfying life. Be in your moments, and you won't regret that you didn't live more intentionally.

I'm giving you permission to let go of whatever's in your past that's tripping you up. Give it a kiss good-bye, then close the door, lock it, and throw away the key! It may sound harsh, but it isn't when you consider that whatever you're paying attention to may actually attract more of this in your future. Do you want your future to be like your past? Do you *really* want that? I think we both know you'd prefer to grow and evolve. Closing the door on the past is like cold water being splashed in your face and saying, "Hey gorgeous! Snap out of that fancy feast you're having on the past and get to the *NOW* of living!" If this speaks to you, you're welcome. We all need to hear that it's OK to let go and move on. Hold your head up and smile…your future awaits!

3. The Ugly Three-Headed Monster

I'm going to be completely transparent here. I have an ugly three-headed monster. Seriously, I really do. It's what makes up my ego, and their names are anger, fear, and hurt. These three have gotten me into loads of trouble as far back as I can remember. Most of my life, I wasn't actually aware they were driving my behavior, beliefs, and attacks on whatever my ego deemed threatening. To make it worse, most things ended up being punishable on some level, whether it was myself or anyone that dared come within one hundred yards of me. It's exhausting trying to live with this ego monster, because no matter how many different ways I tried to appease it, there was no winning. It is, and has always been, a losing game. That is, until I discovered the monster and began calling the three heads out regularly over their sneaky shenanigans. Boundaries and limits were my way back to sanity.

Through asking some tough questions, during my meditation I began to hear the answers. Here's how it worked. Anger, the little devil, would basically act out whenever I felt oppressed or suppressed. The problem was I often didn't speak up to let someone even know what that truth was. This acting out took the form of resentment toward whatever or whoever I felt was suppressing me. I'd stew in it as it consumed my focus in a toxic way. If I had to add up all the time I spent stuck in this pointless cycle, it would probably make me cry.

Looking back, I can see that, growing up, I had an extremely difficult time expressing my truth. I got very good at suppressing it. I believed on an unconscious level that I needed to in order to be *good*, but that was naïve to say the least. First, I believed I was to never question what I was told. Second, I was to not speak my mind, especially if it would upset anyone. So instead I tried to be nice, quiet, and not make waves. I actually believed this ability to suppress made me strong. For years, this meant I wouldn't speak up, say what I wanted or needed, or do or say anything that could upset people. It became extremely challenging to be authentic, because I was too busy trying to be nice. Can you see where this is going?

Here's the no-win part: when I didn't speak up and suppressed how I felt, I got angry A LOT! Oddly, I didn't even know I was angry. Instead, the anger lied to me and told me I was unprotected. Because I believed my wants and needs were unprotected, I blamed others when they couldn't read my mind and give me what I wanted or needed. Talk about crazy! My anger was like an assassin. Because I had no boundaries for this part of my ego, I had issues with trust and put up a huge wall. For many years, I hid behind this wall, believing it was protecting me. As for the outside world, I wore my *nice face*. Can you relate to this? It took me a long time of being willing to get honest with myself before I understood this exhausting cycle I'd grown used to.

When I began to realize what I was doing, my new goal was to do the very thing I was most uncomfortable doing: express my truth. Every time I started asking for what I wanted and needed, I became a little more empowered, and the head of anger became less necessary. Sometimes people could give me what I wanted or needed, and sometimes they couldn't. What was freeing was that I no longer had to wear the "nice face" as a mask to cover up my fear of expressing my truth. What I realized was that, in some ways, the head of anger drew attention to what needed to be healed. I couldn't see this when I was younger, but as I became more willing to look at the ways I sabotaged myself in relationships, I was able to surrender lovingly into the truth.

While I've gotten much better at expressing over the years, it's still something I have to be aware of, simply because it's so darn easy for me to go into "nice mode" without even realizing I'm doing it. Relationships have been a very fertile ground for practice. Many times I've failed, but when I have success in whatever small form, I'm able to step away from the nice face and show my real face. That's progress. Whether I always get it right or not is no longer the point. Making progress by asking for a miracle whenever I find myself falling into an old pattern helps steer my mind back to love. When I'm angry, I'm reacting and not creating my life intentionally. Knowing that the miracle of changing my mind is always available when I ask helps me to know I am supported, protected, and powerful.

Sometimes, behind some our negative ways of handling life, there is a piece of how we learned to cope when we were young. You can speak to this piece of yourself and ask it questions during quiet meditation.

The second head's name is fear. This head has many versions, but one I'm familiar with is the feeling that I will never find someone who truly loves me totally and completely. Unconditional, *Titanic* kind of love. The head of anger and the head of fear collaborated to create many unsatisfying thoughts and feelings. The silent lie that became a frequent whisper was "I'm alone."

This head of fear got the best of me for many years. I believed that, in order to get the love I craved, I once again just had to be "nice enough." *Oh boy, here we go with that again*! But seriously, while my beliefs continued to be distorted, with how to get my wants and needs met, my ego only grew stronger! The truth is, the head of fear kept me small and stopped me from being the best version of myself. It stopped me from shining my light.

Of course, when we experience fear, we believe it's real. That's the crazy part … believing something's real that's not. So around and around this lie goes. That I wasn't *this* enough, or *that* enough. As we think, so shall we be, which meant it was no wonder that I attracted situations and relationships that confirmed this lie. Until I asked for a miracle. I craved to see the truth, and as usual, in meditation I went to the place inside that has answers. For this particular head of my ego, I believed that to be loved I had to be perfect. Or at least to as close to perfect as possible. This set me up for another lesson about showing up as what I thought someone wanted to see versus being able to just be authentically me.

The boundary I used in this area was to simply put self-love, respect, and appreciation first. I stopped looking to the outside for validation and began learning ways to give it to myself. Once I grew comfortable in my own skin, whether someone liked or loved me no longer mattered. I found me. I met me on a totally different level than I'd previously known, and I liked what I found. The need to be perfect had always been an illusion that I bought into when I was young. Letting this lie go helped me gain another piece of freedom and peace. I could just be me. That was enough. It really had always been enough. Whenever the head of fear rises its head, I remember that there's a part of me that's far removed from being judged by any standards of this world. I come from the same place that miracles do. You do too. And when my mind goes somewhere where peace and love are not, I simply ask for the miracle of seeing with love.

My boundary is to no longer entertain lies as reality. To recognize my own worth was a big step in seeing the head of fear for the smoke and mirror show it really was. I know now that I could never possibly be alone. The same spirit connects us all. It may have different faces, but the light in our spirits shines. As we become more open to the light, we are able to let that light shine.

The third head is called hurt. This head's one sneaky mutha! It's the part of my ego that encouraged me to be the victim. When things didn't work out in one way or another, this head of hurt would give me justification to live in my disappointments. It was not a quick kind of sad. More like deep sadness over the "fact" that nothing would ever be that great, so stay small and don't aim too high. The kind that says, "Get in bed and pull the covers over your head, because what's the use?" The lie said, "I'm empty." Ever feel empty? It's so awful. It takes hope and squeezes the life out of it. It takes faith and pees on it. It takes love and rolls its eyes at it.

The head of hurt was the ultimate pessimist. It kept me from truly believing that good opportunities, relationships, success, and anything that would make my heart truly happy was only for other people. This part of my ego exhausted me. It was the "poor me" supporter. Looking back, I can see just how often this head of hurt made me not even want to try. I believed the lie that my life was empty, and guess what I attracted? More feelings of emptiness.

Getting to know the head of anger and the head of fear, it isn't surprising that the head of hurt also played the game of lies so well. Getting honest was again my first step. I asked for the same miracle I always ask for—a change in my perception—and my answer came. The head of hurt was ultimately one of the biggest lies I had to kick to the curb. The truth is, disappointment can't hurt me unless I give it power. I'd given it way too much energy and power for way too long.

Now, when I feel disappointed I know it's time to grow. It's time to raise my standard. It's time to improve, learn something, and get better. It has nothing to do with outside of me, because my beliefs (whether true or not) ALWAYS come from in my mind. Because of this, I have boundaries and limits that set me up to find a positive, successful state. I don't let myself see the worst part of a situation any more. Even if I experience sadness, I know that in every experience I can glean some value. There are many angles to anything. What I've often found is that when there's a disappointment, there's also a huge growth opportunity. I've learned to ask questions within the disappointment. It transforms from a negative to something valuable. Making the choice of what you focus on in *any* situation can make the difference from listening to the head of hurt, or moving forward as a better version of you.

I hope you can see a pattern here. These parts of our egos wreak havoc in our lives. When you begin to put down boundaries and limits, you begin to recognize when your ego's acting up and can begin redirecting your attention to that which better serves you.

4. Keeping First Things First

There is this little thing called multitasking that I believe can be our downfall. As an entrepreneur, I've come to the realization that one person simply cannot do it all *and* keep first things first. First, there is the work I do to make a living. This includes marketing, website updates, newsletters, keeping up with continuing education, doing the actual work itself in a valuable way, scheduling, handling payments, and a plethora of other actions. Then there are family obligations, including spending quality time, giving rides, shopping for family members' needs, and doing all the things that we do because we love our kids. After that there's working out, meal prepping, walking the dog, writing, reading, meditating, seeing friends, seeing family, and on and on. While all this is good, what happens when you're trying to get your shit together and can't seem to come up for air? It's frustrating when you can't seem to scrape up enough time to feel like you're making the kind of progress you'd envisioned when you first set out to create the best version of yourself.

As I write this, I have a huge frustration around the clutter in my home. I hate clutter. It physically affects me when I walk into my office and see a pile of old mail I need to shred. It plain annoys me. So why not just get rid of this pile? For today, it's a time thing. That kind of sounds like an excuse, but it's true. There are a million and one things I do, from the time I wake till I go to bed, but this week this particular pile of clutter hasn't been on the list. What's important gets done first. When I made finishing this book my goal, I decided to make it my *first thing*. So I'm writing because that's my first thing. My first thing isn't clutter. After I write, I'll work out, pick up my daughter, make something to eat, and then I have a few more clients later. After this, my energy will have shifted. I don't know about you, but at the end of the day, I don't want to think about this stack of papers to shred. I'd rather read and see my daughter.

The boundary and limit regarding keeping your first things first means you'll make progress toward what matters most. I'm not saying you won't get to the other things at some point, but it's more important to make a priority of getting your most important things done *first*.

If you don't get the most important things done first, other things have a way of taking over your time. All of a sudden you're tired or hungry, or you get some interruption that'll require hours of your time—and just like that, *your most important thing never gets done*. It just happened! Someone just called as I'm writing this. I'm serious about focusing my time. No means no. Things can wait.

Losing out on making progress toward my most important thing became unacceptable to me. I lost so many days, and it happened to me so many times, that finally I drew the line. Sure, sometimes things like clutter annoy me, but I'm one person. You're one person. Your dreams are yours.

Nobody else is going to make your dreams come true for you. It's something you've got to make a priority.

5. Your Heart

Setting boundaries and limits with your heart is something I wish I'd learned years ago. Our hearts house the seat of our spirits. A broken heart is a broken spirit. How we feel about ourselves is strongly influenced by the people we surround ourselves with. Years ago, I was in love with someone who I felt really broke my heart. It felt shattered in a million pieces. I cried and walked in nature a lot. I sobbed on the floor sometimes. When I walked in nature, I wished the ground would open up and hold me until my heart could breathe again. I didn't know if I'd ever feel right again. Ever feel like your heart hurts so bad it's hard to breathe? Well, thankfully I can't recall many times I've had this experience, but when I did it took me over three years to fully get my heart back. Life went on, of course, but for a long time I carried a heaviness. No one could see it, but I felt it. Because I cared so much, I needed to feel the pain fully so it could leave when the grief period was over.

I bring up this story up because, when I look back, there were red flags all over the place. Maybe because I was young, I thought my heart was invincible, but boy, did I find out I was wrong. I learned it was my job to set boundaries and limits when it comes to my heart.

In the Bible, Proverbs 4:23 says, *"Above all else, guard your heart, for everything you do flows from it."*

Your heart is where your treasure is. A happy heart brings life. A heavy heart makes life darker. Learning to place boundaries and limits is about loving yourself. It's about knowing what lifts you up and helps you shine. Some people, places, and things will help you become the best version of yourself. Be thankful for these gifts and absorb as much as you can from their energy. But there are times in everyone's life when you've got to cut out the weeds that are choking the good. If you're making these decisions, get as much support as you can. Make appointments to see your good friends, visit your therapist, take long walks in nature, get a puppy, buy a good journal to write in, take a course to change your mind, join a hiking group, or do whatever you need to do to feel supported as you prune people, places, or things out of your life. Remember that when you open space for what is no longer serving you, better people, places, and things will have a chance to fill it. There is no lack in the Universe!

One of my favorite requests to the Universe is this: please open the doors that will be good for me and close the ones that won't. We don't always have the awareness if something is good or not for us. This happens so easily sometimes because we get caught up in our *idea of what we want something to be.*

When I was in that relationship years ago, I had a picture of how much this guy loved me and convinced myself he didn't really mean to be abusive to me. I told myself so many lies and made so many excuses. With hindsight, I can see that my idea of love was screwed up and I just didn't know what I didn't know. Thankfully, getting older, I've stopped making up stories and started listening to my heart.

My friend Nancy's "full body yes" test is all I need now. I can feel what's good for me and what's not. The energy of a thing creates a reaction inside of you. You can feel it as either expansive or contracting. When you have boundaries and limits with your heart, you listen to it and protect it. Of course, life is full of lessons, and the lessons of the heart are usually ones we never forget.

You can learn to travel through life surrounded by love, light, and peace. These can be felt directly in your heart. Make it a practice to surround yourself with people, places, and things that reflect the love, respect, and best version of yourself.

WRAP UP

Having boundaries and limits means some things get on your plate and some things don't. You must look at this simple clarity in every area of your life in order to be the best version of you. This is not about making everyone else happy, because you can't. Happiness is an inside job. It's one that we all must take full responsibility for if we are to take back the power of our minds and our lives.

As you start to comb through the different areas of your life, you may see that some are depleted after having no boundaries and limits for far too long. It's OK! Life is all about contrast. It's good to know how you've been trading away your time and energy and what you'll no longer tolerate in order to become a better version of yourself. When you realize how powerful you are to create change in ANY area of your life you can then begin to see that you've always decided either for or against your happiness. You simply can't eat junk food and feel awesome. You simply can't not exercise and feel energized and strong.

Imagine you are president and CEO of a very valuable company. This company is called Your Life. You've been off traveling for some time and have now returned to see how your company is doing. You set up meetings to go over every area and department of your company. You are going to specifically meet with who's been running every department. You begin to see that fear, anger, procrastination, laziness, excuses, poor behavior, and rotten attitudes are running areas of your business. As the one in charge who can make executive decisions, you decide it's time to reestablish some important boundaries and limits. Some of these thoughts that have been running the show need to go if you are to save your company from sabotage! It's uncomfortable to think that you're going to need to fire these thoughts, so you bring in your judge. Your judge is your intuitive and heart-centered "knowing" about the true nature of which thoughts *are or are not* bringing you closer to the best version of you.

Bring each and every thought before the judge. The judge will look down from behind his bench and ask, ***"Did you come from intelligence and love?"*** This question serves you because many of the thoughts we allow to linger in our minds and control our lives come from fear. When we begin to question whether our thoughts come from intelligence and love, we can begin to see their root. When the root is fear, the thought is not serving you. When you do find these kinds of thoughts running areas of your life, learn to question them.

With this kind of visualization, you are also able to see your thoughts from a different perspective, making it easier to see what boundaries and limits you are able to choose. When I first thought of this, I had the judge have the police take the fearful, untrue thoughts to jail. Even a deep subject such as renewing your mind and choosing your thoughts can be made easier with a little humor. We must learn that, at the end of the day, we only have so many days given to us. How we want to spend those days and the quality we wish to experience comes directly from the types of thoughts we allow to circulate and have dominance.

Boundaries and limits say NO in a complete sentence. They also say YES to being the best version of yourself. They say YES to upgrading and leveling up. They say YES to new doors, opportunities, and challenges. It's exciting to begin to take back what is rightfully yours: your life. It's important to decide what gets to stay and what needs to leave. Have peace of mind that you can trust how you feel and that your path to happiness lies right inside YOU.

Boundaries and limits work. Do the work. It's not easy work because no one trained us when we were young to take control of our greatest gift, our minds. Remember that nothing good comes easy, but the rewards equal the work. You're worth whatever it takes to set those boundaries and limits so you can create more time and energy to work on the things that inspire and fulfill you.

LESSON 9 ASSIGNMENT

1. List five areas in your life that could use some healthier boundaries and limits:

   1. _____

   2. _____

   3. _____

   4. _____

   5. _____

Sheryl Corriveau

2. List five advantages you will experience with your time and energy with these boundaries and limits in place:

1. _____

   _____

2. _____

   _____

3. _____

   _____

4. _____

   _____

5. _____

   _____

THE LESSON OF MIRACLES

This existence of ours is as transient as autumn clouds. To watch the birth and death of beings is like looking at the movements of dance. A lifetime is like a flash of lightening in the sky, rushing by like a torrent down a steep mountain.

—Deepak Chopra

My most treasured weapon is access to miracles. I say *weapon* because miracles have been a way out of the fearful world I had created for myself and believed in for far too long. For many years, I believed so strongly in my fears and insecurities that I identified myself with them as facts. When I learned that anything is only real when we believe it, my whole thought system came into question.

A huge turning point happened in my life when, years ago, I found *A Course in Miracles*. It's a metaphysical textbook for students and teachers that points a way out of the fearful thought system of the ego that we've created. When I started reading *A Course in Miracles* (ACIM), I wanted to throw the book across the room! It basically said that the fears I believed in weren't real. *What?* That I'd basically forgotten my true identity. I learned that my true identity had never changed, nor could it, no matter how many fearful lies I'd *chosen* to believe. It said that my identity, and yours, is love. Because we are as we've been created, and we are connected to our Creator, only love is real. Whoa. I had so many feelings as I read these lessons in ACIM, ranging from angry to relieved to totally overwhelmed as to how I was going to rebuild my entire thought system! It's hard to change what you've put a lifetime into creating and upholding. The good news is, we have miracles.

Merriam-Webster's dictionary defines a miracle as "an extraordinary even manifesting diving intervention in human affairs."

The miracle is a shift in the mind from fear to love.

You have access to miracles too. We all do. Unfortunately, many of us weren't taught this. For over eight years, I've been a student in A Course in Miracles. In studying its principles, I'm come to realize that, all along, I've had access to my Higher Power (God, Source, Love). With this access, whenever I realize I've lost my peace, I can ask for a miracle. The miracle always brings me back to the truth. We all fight this battle, until we realize we don't have to.

The truth is love. You are love. I am love. We all are love. When we drift, the miracle brings us back to the truth. The battle of the mind is between thoughts of love vs. fear. Fear takes your power away. Our egos use fear to keep us small and prevent us from being the best version of ourselves. Miracles are our way out of fear. Our job is to remember to *ask*.

FIVE QUESTIONS TO SHOW YOU NEED A MIRACLE

1. Does fear get you in a headlock, preventing you to step out as your authentic self?

2. Is your self-talk negative in terms what you're capable of being, doing, or having?

3. Have you stopped trying to improve in certain areas because you don't believe you can?

4. Do you look to things outside of yourself in order to feel good?

5. Do you wish could feel more peace, love, and joy?

No matter where you are on your journey, learning to lean on miracles will change your life. In this chapter, we'll dive deep into how to use miracles to create more meaningful love, joy, and peace. You aren't alone in whatever you're seeking to change. In any area, your perception can completely turn around. If you're willing to choose differently.

FIVE METHODS TO CREATING MIRACLES

1. Understand the Miracle

According to ACIM, the ego believes that power, understanding, and truth lie in separation from each other. To establish this belief it must attack. When operating from this place, fear is dominant and love has left the building. When you come to a point in life where being true to yourself is more important than feeding the ego, you're ready for a miracle. Preferring love over fear, peace over anxiety, and joy over separation is what the miracle is all about. ACIM says it best: "Do I want the problem, or do I want the answer?"

The miracle isn't outside of us. We don't need to beg for it. You simply learn to offer everything you don't want to your holy inner guide (ACIM calls it the Holy Spirit). Then ask for a miracle. I don't think there's a day now when I *don't* ask for a miracle. Often, it's during mediation, when I'm taking inventory on whatever's going on inside me. But I also ask whenever I lose my peace, attack and separate myself in some way, hear the voice of fear, or simply deter from love, peace, and joy. It's a practice that I've grown to love, because it means I'm never stuck in a bad neighborhood of my mind's creation. It's my instant pass to freedom.

When I truly turn within and ask for a miracle, it always comes. At first this was challenging because I'd grown accustomed to hearing my ego's voice, but as I kept practicing hearing my inner guide's voice, it became more familiar. For miracles, it's for your Inner Spirit's voice that you must learn to hear. It doesn't yell. It won't scream at you. It's never negative, fearful, or unintelligent. It's a voice of love, and it speaks to the truth that you are and always have been. It's the voice of the companion given to you by God. When you begin to ask, be ready to receive miracles.

Receiving miracles is different for everyone. Sometimes I'll get a hit of intuition, sometimes it's a peaceful feeling or another way of looking at a situation, an idea to go for a walk, a song or podcast, a friend randomly calling with some insight, or any number of ways Spirit can reach you. It's easy to think of yourself as separate from Source, but you are intimately connected to this masterful guide within you. Learning how to cultivate this relationship works the same as any other. It's about asking and *listening*. Spending quiet time in meditation. This is really to quiet your ego's voice. Making your spiritual relationship a priority is what it comes down to.

2. Being Who You Are Now

I used to grapple with the question, "Who did I think I was to be a miracle-minded person when I'd done so many *bad* things?" Did you hear my ego's voice there? Bad, dumb, stupid, wrong, should have, awful, etc.… these are all accusations from the ego. They will come up as you lean into the best version of yourself. Why? Because the ego doesn't want to be wrong, so it makes *you* wrong. If you go toward love, peace and joy, inevitably you'll hear this voice of ego.

Some of my egos questions included: "How can you be so selfish running your own business when you could be spending time with your daughter?" Or, "How can someone like you when you've made so many mistakes, still think you deserve miracles?!"

Whatever your ego can use against you for, it will. The good news is that you have a choice which voice you listen to. *Choice* is the key. I used to think I didn't have a choice. This is why ACIM literally saved my life. My faulty, fearful thinking was running rampant, ruling parts of my life like a narcissist dictator. At the beginning of my journey inward, I quickly realized there was a serious lack of order in my mind. My thoughts ran like wild mustangs. It is frightening to feel out of control. So I did what many people do: I distracted myself. There is no shortage of ways we do this, including drinking, sex, drugs, food, shopping, television, social media, etc. Distraction seemed to work…until it didn't. I wanted to be at peace and feel good inside. And I didn't. This is when I found ACIM and slowly began realizing we are all entitled to miracles. There *was* a way out of my fearful thinking.

What gave me hope was that I didn't have to conjure up a miracle using my *own strength*. That's the beauty of it. It comes from a wiser, truthful, and loving place, whether you call it God, Universe, Source, or Higher Power.

When you experience a miracle, you'll realize that a shift has taken place in your mind. You will realize you didn't do this on your own. A miracle is your spiritual answer for your desire to choose love over fear. It's a miracle because it enables us to move past the lies and fears. Our way back to who we really are is one miracle at a time. It's our way back to love.

3. Ask, Ask, Ask

This is your part. Asking isn't something I'd often think to do, until I'd gone around and around in my mind, finally realizing I still wasn't feeling better about whatever had my attention. I'm not going to lie—in the beginning, it felt a little strange to ask for a miracle.

> "Inner guide, I need a miracle. Please help change how I'm seeing this situation. Please help me choose love. I'm open to your guidance. Thank you."

To this day, when I ask, I keep it simple. I still say please and thank you. I don't make it complicated because that's my usual problem. Complications come from the ego. When you hear your inner guide speak, it's peaceful. It brings sanity to your ego's insanity.

So that's your job: Ask. Wait and listen. Meditate if you can. Go on a long walk in nature and embrace the silence. Learn to be still in order to hear.

ACIM says there is no order of difficulty in miracles. One is not "harder" or "bigger" than another. They are all the same. All expressions of love are maximal.

Miracles occur naturally as expressions of love. The real miracle is the love that inspires them. In this sense, everything that comes from love is a miracle.

All miracles mean life, and God is the Giver of Life. His voice will direct you very specifically. You will be told all you need to know.

Realizing we are all connected to our Creator, and to each other, cannot help but change our perceptions of separation and conflict. Asking for a miracle is natural, because you are asking to be reminded of the truth. And the truth is love. Since you are love, and a miracle is an expression of love, asking simply becomes choosing to see the truth about who you really are.

As you cultivate your relationship to your inner guide through asking for and receiving miracles, you will be drawn to the light. This light is where you came from and where you still belong. Wandering in the darkness for so long, is what made me so hungry for the light. If this resonates with you, your spirit is calling you back to the light. All's that's necessary is a willingness to set your ego aside in exchange for truth. You don't need to know everything, just ask and it will be given. Doing this daily will change your life.

4. Don't Make a Mountain Out of a Mistake

Any other perfectionistic, control freaks out there? This was a big lesson I needed to learn. I'd start changing for the better, and then I'd screw up in some way. My ego, which is always doing push-ups in the bushes, absolutely revels when I make a mistake! It could go on the attack at a second's notice. It's exhausting to let my ego beat me up! Do you know what I mean? It is the voice of fear, shame, condemnation, guilt, and other self-deprecating accusations. It can undo all the good you've been working toward with one violent swing.

Eventually, I began to see my mistakes for what they really were. Mistakes.

ACIM sums it up nicely: "The Holy Spirit is not delayed in his teaching by your mistakes. He can be held back only by your unwillingness to let them go. Let us therefore be determined, particularly for the next week or so, to be willing to forgive ourselves for our lapses in diligence, and our failures to follow the instructions for practicing the day's idea. This tolerance for weakness will enable us to overlook it, rather than give it power to delay our learning. If we give it power to do this, we are regarding it as strength, and are confusing strength with weakness."

This means that when you mess up, forgive yourself and move on. Dwelling on past mistakes keeps you stuck. It's a choice. Acknowledge whatever it is that happened, but don't beat yourself up over it. There's a big difference in those two ways of handling mistakes. We don't stop making mistakes just because we're adults. Our egos have just had undisciplined reign over our minds for so long that making different choices about how we see ourselves has simply never come into question. This book has been all about making different choices about how you see yourself.

Remember that making mistakes is how we learn and grow. If I hadn't made so many mistakes in my life, I wouldn't have realized the kind of person I wanted to be. Look at your mistakes as opportunities to give you strength. They give you a chance to know who you are, what you can rise from, and how you can still come out of it.

5. See Things Not as They Are—But as They Can Be

The potential in you is unlimited. We all need to work on this truth. In real estate, there are many run-down houses for sale. Some buyers look and see nothing but a run-down house. Other buyers have a vision of what the home could look like if they fixed this and did that. It's all in whether you are seeing things as they are now, or as they can be. The same is true for your life. Some parts may need some work. Heck, maybe a lot of parts do! But guess what? You're the perfect person for the job! Life's going to happen one way or the other, so why not work to improve yourself?

The other day I was thinking about how fast the month of July goes by. I'm not sure why, but July just seems to fly by for me. Then I was thinking how, in four years, my daughter will be graduating high school. That's only four Julys! For some reason, seeing there are only four Julys in four years seemed pretty short! The truth is, sometimes we forget how fast life does go by. These thoughts made me realize how much I want to accomplish before these four Julys are over. It put a different lens on what I want and need to do in order to make my goals real. It makes me want to get moving toward it today!

Whatever you see in yourself, remember there is always potential that you don't see. You're a soul housed in a body that has been given to you as a gift. We mistake our bodies for our true identities. Love is our real identity. Let light shine away anything that prevents your true sight. Pray you may see the gift of life you've been given. All the best gifts can't be bought in a store, including your children, health, life, peace, love, joy, inner beauty, giving, laughter, kindness, breath, time, forgiveness, allowing, wisdom, quiet, and listening. These are soul qualities that make our souls smile.

You aren't here to do nothing. You're here to be the light you were meant to be. You can do that by asking for miracles as you work on becoming the very best version of yourself possible!

WRAP UP

The Universe doesn't work the way we often perceive it. Let me ask you a question: do you make changes in your comfort zone or out of it? Most of us are creatures of comfort.

There have been times when it felt as if the rug was pulled out from under me. It's not comfortable…but it wakes you up to other aspects of yourself. You do things you hadn't done before. You may start asking for miracles and get tight with Spirit. You may need to let go of some things. You may need to do or learn some things you wouldn't have. To grow and stretch hurts until we let go and give ourselves to that moment. It is a surrender, but I've learned to assist myself by saying thank you. Everyone who has pushed themselves to the point when every fiber in their being wants to quit but they don't, *knows* these are the moments that the greatest change takes place. When life is the most challenging is often when the greatest changes are happening to make you better.

LESSON 10 ASSIGNMENT

1. If you look ahead to your next four Julys, what do you want to accomplish in terms of being, doing, and having?

   _____

   _____

2. In what area of your life do you need a miracle?

   _____

   _____

LAST WORDS

People want someone to lead who gives them hope to be better themselves. You have an opportunity to do just that. During your time on Earth, you're invited to become the very best version of yourself possible. It's about your reputation *to yourself*. If you say yes to this invitation, you become a source of what's possible. No matter what setbacks you've had, it's the comeback that really matters. When you become authentic and free, when you show up in the world being totally yourself, you're a force of light that changes this planet. When you live your life intentionally, following whatever your heart and soul have been calling for you to become, you cannot help but inspire others. Squeeze all you can from every day. Make your moments matter. Live with no regrets. Always ask for a miracle.

Sat nam.

ABOUT THE AUTHOR

Along with being an author, Sheryl Corriveau is also an inspirational speaker, entrepreneur, Pilates/NASM personal trainer, IIN & TYL (Transform Your Life) Coach, and Realtor. She uses her enthusiasm and creativeness through teaching, writing, and speaking to help inspire others to become empowered and confident to rise up and live the best version of themselves.

www.SherylCorriveau.com
Instagram: @SherylCorriveau

Made in the USA
Columbia, SC
27 October 2018